THE **BRISKET** BOOK

A Love Story with Recipes

STEPHANIE PIERSON

Photographs by
Roger Sherman

**Andrews McMeel
Publishing, LLC**
Kansas City · Sydney · London

The Brisket Book

Andrews McMeel Publishing, LLC
an Andrews McMeel Universal company
1130 Walnut Street, Kansas City, Missouri 64106
www.andrewsmcmeel.com

11 12 13 14 15 WKT 10 9 8 7 6 5 4 3 2 1
ISBN: 978-1-4494-0697-4
Library of Congress Control Number: 2011921500

Edited by Dorothy Kalins, Dorothy Kalins Ink, LLC
Design and illustrations by Happy Menocal

ATTENTION: SCHOOLS AND BUSINESSES
Andrews McMeel books are available at quantity discounts
with bulk purchase for educational, business, or sales
promotional use. For information, please e-mail the
Andrews McMeel Publishing Special Sales Department:
specialsales@amuniversal.com

To Eric: More tender than . . .

To Phoebe and Hazel. To Megan and Lucy.
I've got the best recipe ever.

To Dorothy Kalins, Editor and Forever Friend:
Thanks for your insight, vision, and brilliance.
Anyone can make a brisket—you can make it sing.

To Roger Sherman: Thank you for bringing this
book to gorgeous juicy life with your
spirited, spontaneous, stylish photographs.

CONTENTS

Cézanne? No, Joan Nathan. This glorious Still Life With Brisket Prep was created in her own kitchen.

Introduction

"In a world of Rachel Zoe makeovers, brisket is completely comfortable with what it isn't."

Some foods will improve your meal, your mood, your day, your buttered noodles. Brisket will improve your life. A well-cooked brisket is meltingly tender, soothing, savory, warming, welcoming.

Brisket isn't some snobby dish you can't pronounce or afford. It's not posh—rarely has a truffle ever gone into the making of one. Culinary expert and food historian Nach Waxman (who seems to have the world's most Googled braised brisket recipe) says, "Brisket is a real family and friends meal. It's not something you'd serve at a grand déjeuner."

In a world of Rachel Zoe makeovers, brisket is completely comfortable with what it isn't. It is "a workhorse meal," says *The New Best Recipe, From the Editors of Cook's Illustrated*, a book that musters up a hell of a lot more enthusiasm for flank steak. Molecular gastronomists have not been able to alter brisket's perfect DNA or turn it into a foam. It's as content bathed in Heinz ketchup as it is nestled in a day-after taco. It's so simple and forgiving that even the worst cook can make a good one. It's a happy interfaith marriage: in Simon Hopkinson's recipe for Boiled Beef and Carrots with Parsley Dumplings and Chrain, brisket is served with classic English dumplings and sauced with a Jewish beetroot and horseradish purée.

Every country, every community, every culture, every family seems to have a brisket recipe. Just the etymology of the word *brisket* is mind-boggling (see page 36). But while there are millions of brisket recipes and thousands of reasons they came to be, there are essentially only three cooking techniques. You can braise a brisket, barbecue it, or brine it so it becomes corned beef. It's that simple.

"Brisket is a crosscultural wonder—a Jewish dish cooked in a Dutch oven with a Sicilian sauce served in North Dakota."

Brisket can be the star of the show or it can play a supporting role, with equal success. Boiled gently, brisket is the key player in a French pot-au-feu. It's a defining ingredient in Italian bollito misto. Alsatians build their choucroute garnie on brisket. In Slavic regions, it's the basis of a great borscht. Eastern Europeans have traditionally cooked it as cholent, a Sabbath stew, and for tzimmes, a fruit or vegetable stew that's served on Rosh Hashanah. Hong Kong noodle soups are often simmered with tender pieces of beef brisket.

Sure, you can gussy a brisket up (Boeuf en Daube à la Provençale à la Julia Child), but a basic brisket requires little more than a few juicy ingredients to keep it from drying out and the patience to wait for it to cook s . . . l . . . o . . . w . . . l . . . y. With an oven temperature that rarely goes above 325°F and a smoker temperature that hovers around 225°F, brisket is not for the Type A gourmet. Cooking time is anywhere from three hours for a braised brisket to thirteen hours in a smoker (a veritable miniature sweat lodge for a properly barbecued brisket) plus overnight time for the rub. Want a corned beef? Expect your brisket to brine for up to six or seven days. Got a lot of time on your hands? Chef Todd Gray's sous vide brisket takes around thirty hours from start to finish. Time and the brisket are friends.

While a braised brisket is like nothing else, it is often confused with its boring cousin, pot roast. A brisket is—in the most literal sense—a "pot roast." That is, a roast that is cooked in a pot. But . . . a pot roast is not necessarily a brisket. The cooking method—braising—is the same for both, but a pot roast can be made with lots of different cuts of meat—sometimes brisket, but more often rump, chuck, or round. So a "pot roast" is a braised beef dish. Bonus round: What's the difference between braising and stewing? Stewing requires more liquid. And braising results in a more concentrated sauce.

Let me just say what you can already feel. I love brisket. I say, a brisket in every pot, in every Crock-Pot, on every Weber, in every barbecue joint, on every Passover platter, in every deli, at every butcher, in every food truck, on every TV food show, food site, food blog.

And I love leftovers. (Brisket Rule #1: Make a Lot. Brisket Rule #2: Make More.) Brisket with biscuits and gravy. Brisket hash. Brisket in an enchilada. Reheated brisket on a slice of challah. Just the fragrant aroma of brisket cooking is delicious—I don't even have to taste it to know how ambrosial and full-out flavorful it will be when it is finally on my plate.

If I am crazy about brisket, I have found out, to my delight, so are millions of others. If you enter "brisket" on the Chowhound

Anyone can go to the bakery for a birthday cake! The founder of noexcusesbbq.com went to his Weber and whipped up this rocking barbecued brisket birthday cake for his daughter.

boards, you'll find a feeding frenzy of posts: "Too Much Leftover Smoked Brisket!" "Should I Have Rinsed the Corned Beef Brisket?" "Stringy Brisket—Why?" "Has Anyone Tried Ina Garten's Brisket?" You would never find such responses for "rump roast" or "chuck" or even "leg of lamb." Then there's the brisket lover in Oregon who "surprised" his daughter with a barbecued brisket "birthday" cake—a large rectangular piece of smoked meat with brightly colored candles stuck in the top. The Obamas served a brisket at their first Passover seder in the White House. There are brisket jokes, brisket cartoons, brisket lyrics, Louis Armstrong YouTube brisket videos. And you don't even have to eat it to love it: "I've heard angels singing when I cut it," confesses a believer.

But for me, the odd rave here and there will just not do it. I believe brisket deserves more. After all, brisket has no powerful lobby like the National Chicken Council. Nothing to rival National Pork Month. Steak has steak houses. Veal has a PR agency. And don't tell brisket, but Chilean sea bass is on Facebook. Worse yet, while almost every cookbook has a brisket, brisket doesn't even have a cookbook. Until now.

Thinly cut and richly sauced, the irresistibly delicious brisket from Nach Waxman. Recipe p.110.

This book—for the first time—explains why brisket, humble in name and origin and certainly no looker, is the ultimate comfort food. This is why it deserves praise, attention, and yes, fame.

Three of the most important things I've learned in my quest to celebrate brisket:

#1: With the exception of competition level pit masters, master chefs, and Ari Weinzweig at Zingerman's in Ann Arbor, just about everyone else believes he or she has the best brisket recipe ever. That's actually the entire dialogue.

ME: "Do you have a brisket recipe?"

PERSON: "Are you kidding?! I have the best recipe ever!"

#2: Extensive, unbiased recipe testing proved that any recipe with "Best" or "Perfect" in the title was neither.

#3: With all due respect, recipes that non-cooks have borrowed from sort-of cooks—like "My Pediatrician's Brisket"—will never win any awards.

During an entire year of brisketeering (I'll confess to obsession), I cooked with and interviewed some of the country's top chefs, cookbook writers, pit masters, home cooks, food historians, butchers, and ranchers. I researched the subject hungrily, in hundreds of cookbooks, history books, culinary memoirs, and tomato sauce—stained archival recipe books. I devoured brisket food blogs, recipe and restaurant reviews; visited chat rooms filled with passionate foodies passionate about their briskets. I traveled from Maine to Kansas City to Baltimore to Brooklyn to eat brisket, and because I love my boyfriend almost as much as I love brisket, I once brought two pounds of still-warm leftovers home from Boston on Jet Blue in the overhead.

The result? Now brisket has its own book. Not just any book: the definitive brisket book. Well, it is the only one after all. (Don't worry, I won't reveal the ending.) But I can share with you the fact that I carefully evaluated the merits of every brisket recipe as well as the intentions of every brisket maker. My method? High hopes. Higher standards. Tender meat and tough love.

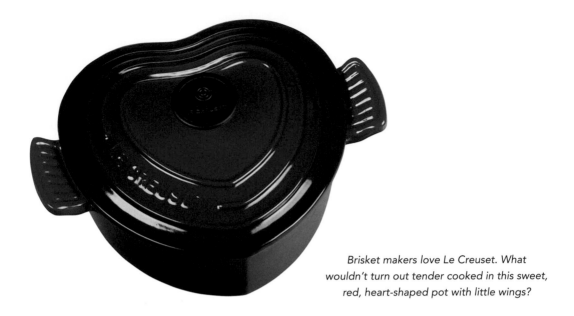

Brisket makers love Le Creuset. What wouldn't turn out tender cooked in this sweet, red, heart-shaped pot with little wings?

I couldn't have done it—and didn't do it—without Kathy Brennan, culinary and editorial collaborator extraordinaire whose impeccable credentials include being a Bert Greene and James Beard Journalism Award winner, stints at *Saveur* and *Gourmet*, and positions in the kitchens of restaurants like Matthew's in New York City and Nicholini's in Hong Kong. Did I mention that Kathy graduated first in her class from The French Culinary Institute?

Let me just say that if you had passed by Kathy's lovely suburban home, just slightly south of Philadelphia anytime in the last ten or so months, you would have died and gone to heaven with the smell of briskets braising in the oven and briskets smoking on the grill out back. Tahini briskets, vegan briskets, braggin' rights briskets. Mmmm . . . And let's hear it for Kathy's devoted family, who started out loving brisket but got just a little tired of it (well, maybe more than a little) after about the fiftieth recipe. In fact, one day, when we were almost done, Kathy's nine-year-old son came home from school, popped into the kitchen, and asked what was for dinner. "Brisket," Kathy told him. And tears welled up in his eyes.

Now, it's back to chicken and flounder for the grateful Brennans. But Kathy and I did what we set out to do: selected recipes that are really, truly, without a doubt, the best brisket recipes ever, each a distinct type. Every single one has been tested and tasted, some more than once. (Hey, Meira Goldberg—how come you didn't tell us that your cholent was *chunks* of meat, not a whole brisket?!) The recipes are straightforward, the headnotes smart, the instructions clear as a bell. And you don't have to go to Sri Lanka for any of the ingredients. It's all happening—okay, maybe not the aquavit or the Korean chile—at the Stop & Shop.

"On an emotional level, you can celebrate with brisket, mourn with it, diet with it, defrost with it, court with it, make a friend with it."

Our winning recipes have won competitions, won hearts, made us smile at their utter simplicity, surprised us with their ingenuity, dazzled us with their flavor, touched us with their devotion to not changing a single thing. It is clear—and wonderful—that there are many different roads to brisket bliss. To quote the Pulitzer Prize—winning poet, Mark Strand, "I raise my fork and I eat."

POT ROAST

a poem by Mark Strand

I gaze upon the roast,

that is sliced and laid out

on my plate

and over it

I spoon the juices

of carrot and onion.

And for once I do not regret

the passage of time.

I sit by a window that looks on the soot-stained brick of buildings and do not care that I see no living thing—not a bird, not a branch in bloom, not a soul moving in the rooms behind the dark panes. These days when there is little to love or to praise one could do worse than yield to the power of food. So I bend

to inhale

the steam that rises

from my plate, and I think

of the first time

I tasted a roast

like this.

It was years ago

in Seabright,

Nova Scotia;

my mother leaned

over my dish and filled it

and when I finished

filled it again.

I remember the gravy,

its odor of garlic and celery,

and sopping it up

with pieces of bread.

And now

I taste it again.

The meat of memory.

The meat of no change.

I raise my fork

and I eat.

from Selected Poems by Mark Strand (Alfred A. Knopf, 1990)

"*Dorothy, could you come here a minute?*"

1 Every Brisket Tells a Story: Provenance and Passion

"Whence could it have come to me, this all-powerful joy?"

—*Marcel Proust*, Remembrance of Things Past, Volume 1

A buttery rich madeleine you could understand. So French, so delicate, so, well . . . so Proustian: "Whence could it have come to me, this all-powerful joy?" But why does a flaccid four-pound, gray-brown piece of beef, shaped roughly like the state of Tennessee, inspire Proustian prose, evoke the deepest pleasure, create indelible memories? I didn't even know what a brisket was until I was about twenty-five years old. My mother never made brisket (can you say, "Vivian, Swedish Lutheran lover of lutefisk?"), but when, years later, I put the first voluptuous piece into my mouth, fork-tender, adrift in a rich, sweet onion gravy, accompanied by supernal mashed potatoes and roasted carrots, well . . . you had me at brisket. (Full disclosure: my father, Mannie, was Jewish, so clearly I have a strong brisket gene.)

Now, when I hear that a friend is cooking a brisket for dinner, I get choked up—a brisket—for me? No, it's too much. You don't need to do that. We'll order Chinese. One of my closest friends revealed the secret ingredient in her family's brisket recipe, and I started to cry. That's the moment I realized that I needed to get to the bottom of why so many of us have such a strong emotional attachment to this sort of blah cut of beef that doesn't even sit anywhere near the sexy sirloin or the fancy filet mignon on a steer. Is it because even a pretty bad cook can turn a brisket into a pretty decent dish or save it from disaster? Does brisket just scream "happy intact family," even when it's not your own family? Is it because while we have lost mother tongues, changed our last names, and moved all over the world, we have somehow managed not to lose our recipes for brisket—recipes that have been handed down and copied and e-mailed and tweeted? (Whose heart wouldn't melt a little hearing about Aunt Irene's New England brisket recipe, which was passed down to her niece Alice, who gave it to her friend Ellen, who shared it with her nephew John, who let his girlfriend—who had never even eaten a brisket—copy it for her mother so she could help her cook it?)

But our passion for brisket goes beyond the recipe or the result. I wondered if there is something to the fact that brisket is just so unpretentious. It has no airs. Not to mention a pretty unimpressive provenance. It did come over early from Europe, but it is one of a very few not to claim that it came over on the Mayflower. Nor was barbecued brisket born with a silver spoon in its mouth. When the breast of a steer was first slow smoked in the hinterlands of South America and/or the Caribbean, it was by people more likely to be called "natives" than "chefs." Or could it be that for years, brisket was so affordable you could serve your whole family, invite the neighbors, set an extra place for the rabbi and his wife, and still have leftovers for a week?

While all these things are true and contribute to its lasting resonance, I believe the real reason for brisket's powerful allure is even simpler. Brisket will be what you want it to be. And that, with all due respect, is more than you can honestly say about your teenager, your hair, your Labradoodle, or most members of Congress. On an emotional level, you can celebrate with it, mourn with it, diet with it, defrost with it, court with it, make a friend with it. Come to think of it, there are very few brisket recipes that do not have the word *love* somewhere in their headnotes or descriptions. On a cooking level, it's a perfect culinary blank canvas, adept at adapting to everything you rub on or throw in, from garlic salt to Liquid Smoke to miso to gingersnaps to huge gulps of Dr Pepper. The Jewish cookbook author Joan Nathan rightly calls brisket the Zelig of meats.

"Please, help my father's old age home hold a wonderful brisket this New Year . . . Help my mother be the envy of her Mah-Jongg group . . . "

—Chowhound post

Le Creuset as supporting player: Some cooks believe that weighing down the meat helps it brown more evenly.

Brisket can be fattening when you want an über-hearty winter meal but it can also be nonfattening, counterintuitive as that may sound. I was shocked to see that there is a Weight Watchers version (Weight Watchers Roasted Brisket), probably the only brisket recipe you will ever see that calls for lean beef. It isn't actually "roasted," by the way. This recipe optimistically (and parsimoniously) suggests that 2½ pounds of brisket will serve eight people. Each serving size is 3 ounces, which is about as big as a man's pocket watch. There is no calorie count because Weight Watchers uses their own system instead, but trust me, this is the brisket you'd invite Kate Moss over for and tell her not even to think about asking for seconds.

Chef Sara Moulton, on the other delicious and decadent hand, throws caution to the wind with her Red-Wine Braised Beef Brisket with Horseradish Sauce. One serving size of what sounds like the brisket of my dreams is a reasonable 6 ounces. The calorie count for this portion is a hefty 1,059. Calories from fat: 664. In trying to see if there is some standard home ec-y calorie count—and knowing we could be talking jumbo potatoes and rich stout as ingredients—I turned to wiki.answers.com, which informed me that "there are approximately 448 to 496 calories in 8 ounces of reasonably lean braised beef brisket." And calorie-conscious fatsecret.com says that a half pound of beef brisket "Flat Half, trimmed to ⅛" fat, Select Grade, Cooked, Braised" has 635 calories. But who's counting?! For the Weight *non*-Watcher, a killer (don't take my word for it, get a second opinion from a cardiologist) "Hot Beef Sundae" is on the Midway menu at the Indiana State Fair—a staggering mountain of corn, mashed potatoes, and something close to what looks like two pounds of marinated brisket, topped with rich beef gravy and festive ribbons of shredded cheese.

And if all this fat, nonfat, caloric talk is making you nervous, good news: there's brisket the way your therapist wants it to be. There are a number of online recipes for Prozac Brisket. Had a bad day? Anxious about your new job? These empathic brisket recipes (none actually made with Prozac) feel and heal your pain with every soothing bite. Fire the therapist and hire the brisket. Of course, since brisket manages to be all things to all people, a brisket for those with low self-esteem is matched by one for those with a healthy ego. In a number of barbecue cookbooks, I found recipes for Braggin' Rights Brisket made with a heap of skills, however you say chutzpah in Texas, and a custom grill/smoker big enough to turn out a couple hundred pounds of brisket, pork butts, and racks of ribs.

A poster on the midway at the Indiana State Fair. It almost seems like health food compared with fried butter or deep-fried peanut butter cups.

"Oh, state fair food! Nothing like a hot beef sundae before a boyz II men concert and a tilt-a-whirl ride."

—*boingboing.net post*

You Transform Brisket. Brisket Transforms You.

Researching the ASBEE competition, I came across a piece from blogger and ASBEE devotee, Steven Weinberger. His title is "Hava NaGrilla! Inside a Kosher BBQ Competition." Which is a) charming and b) makes you wonder whether kosher Jews have some extra punning gene. An excerpt: "That weekend we weren't the Weinbergers from NY (although that was impressive to many of the locals). We were 'Fleish Gordon and his Beefy Bunch'—fleish, meaning 'meat' in Yiddish. I was Fleish Gordon, in a red costume with golden yellow cape. My wife was 'Princess Paprika.' My children were 'Brisket Boy,' 'BarB-Cutie,' 'The Ribster,' 'Beanie,' and 'Lil' Sauce.' We were Intergalactic Barbecue Heroes, on a mission to spread good eating . . . I'm glad to say that I was the adult pickle eating champion this year . . ."

"Fleish Gordon" working his superpowers at the kosher barbecue competition in Memphis, Tennessee.

When I go to a ballgame, personally, I root for the food. So, it seems do Los Angeles Angels fans. In a tight race (food, not pennant), locally sourced Beach Pit BBQ's brisket sandwich was introduced to Anaheim Stadium and promptly won a national contest for best ballpark cuisine. Way to go, Aramark Chef Marco Garcia! The headline in the *Orange County Register* says it all: "Brisket rules: Hot dog no longer king at Angel Stadium." The *New York Times* hailed Chef Garcia's sandwich as "must-order ballpark cuisine" and the *Register* called it "Ballpark Food of the Gods." Parenthetically, if you are serving a crowd, this is probably the only brisket recipe that will feed 45,281. You want big league? Check. You want devout? Check. Check. At the annual ASBEE (an acronym for the name of a local synagogue) Kosher BBQ Contest and Festival in Memphis, brisket is one of the main draws. This year, more than forty teams competed and over 3,000 kosher barbecue mavens from all over the country attended. Who cares who won the cooking competition? The LeBron Flames and the Miami Meat Team from the Margolin

Angel Stadium in Anaheim, California, where discerning fans prefer brisket.

"Brisket rules: Hot dog no longer king at Angel Stadium!"

—The Orange County Register

Hebrew Academy of Memphis won awards for both the best booth and the best name. However, my personal blue ribbon goes to a team called The Rabbi and his Bris-Kit, led by Rabbi Levi Klein of Chabad Lubavitch of Tennessee. It turns out that Rabbi Klein is a mohel, hence the team motto: "The tip's on us." Oy.

You want to marry outside your faith? Here comes the brisket . . . Love, honor, and cherish take on delicious new meaning. According to a *New York Times* article I read, Paul O'Connell, chef/owner of Chez Henri in Cambridge, Massachusetts, was inspired by his Jewish girlfriend to make his first brisket. Her family absolutely loves it. His brisket starts with a spice rub, is first grilled, then braised with onions, mustard, and Worcestershire sauce. After that, Chef O'Connell is grilled by his girlfriend's family. Why, they want to know, can't he add prunes and dried apricots like they do? Chef O'Connell, a happy and successful brisket convert, observes, "I see great compatibility with Irish and Jewish cooking. In both traditions you slowly braise meats and vegetables together so that toothless grandmothers can chew them."

Another recent brisket believer is Todd Gray, chef and co-owner of Washington, D.C.'s award-winning Equinox Restaurant, who converted some of *his* cooking when he married his Jewish wife—and Equinox co-owner—Ellen Kassoff Gray. He told me, "Brisket has always been a back-seat type of cut for me. When I was challenged to cook it for my father-in-law, my wife said, 'Why not put it on the menu for the holidays?' Which I did—and it's been a huge success. So I've done it as a classic braise." I was lucky enough to sample this brisket and learned how Chef Gray prepares it for diners at his restaurant. Since his sophisticated patrons demand top quality, outstanding flavor, and an artfully prepared dish, this is no casual home-cooked brisket. We're not at Aunt Irene's anymore. Both taste and presentation are showcased. After Chef Gray cooks his brisket, he presses the meat down with heavy weights in the kitchen. He explains that by pressing it, you tighten it down . . . the piece of brisket becomes more dense. It also makes it easier for him to cut into neat cubes. When served on the plate, the meat practically cuts itself and, perhaps because it comes from Virginia grass-fed, grain-finished cattle, it manages to be both rich and tender, neither too lean nor too fat. Chef Gray's sauce, like none that I have experienced, is reduced to a thick glossy glaze that lets all the flavor shine through.

Proving that brisket welcomes all faiths, be they ever so jumbled, there is also a juicy Jews for Jesus recipe. Jews for Jesus, meet Vegetarians for Brisket. Yes, while the idea of a vegetarian brisket might seem like a contradiction in terms, even people who don't like meat like brisket. So they make it their own with warmly satisfying vegetarian alternatives like a vegan seitan corned beef, a barbecued portobello brisket, a seitan braised brisket. Tradition! But what if you are a totally 100 percent committed vegetarian who occasionally eats a piece of meat on the down-low?

Women of a certain age solving the world's problems.

"I see great compatibility with Irish and Jewish cooking.
In both traditions you slowly braise meats and vegetables
together so that toothless grandmothers can chew them."

—*Chef Paul O'Connell, owner Chez Henri, Cambridge, Massachusetts*

Head down to New Orleans where Taceaux Loceaux, a local street food vendor, serves a meat lovers' brisket taco called Messin' with Texas and a non-meat version called All Hat, No Cattle. Then there is the most enchanting title of all, from Los Angeles vegan cookbook writer, actress, and blogger, Jenn Shagrin: Vegan Peppercorn and Red Wine Braised Brisket and Jelly Donut Twinkies.

Here's a very terrific seitan brisket recipe with nary a Ring Ding in sight.

Starring miso, brown sugar, and caraway seeds

A SEÏTAN BRÏSKET

Adapted from Leah Koenig, MyJewishLearning.com

Serves 4–6

You don't need beef to make a sprightly, satisfying brisket. When making the gravy, it's easier to stir the flour into the fat, switching to a whisk when you add in the broth.

VEGETABLES AND SEITAN

2	tablespoons olive oil
2	medium onions, peeled and sliced vertically into ½-inch pieces
2	medium carrots, peeled and sliced into 1-inch pieces
2	celery stalks, sliced into 1-inch pieces
½	tablespoon tamari
15	ounces seitan, sliced into 6 pieces

GLAZE

1½	tablespoons grape juice or fruity red wine
2	tablespoons brown sugar
1½	tablespoons miso paste

GRAVY

1¾	cups "no chicken" chicken stock or vegetable stock, plus extra if necessary
¾	cup grape juice or fruity red wine
1½	tablespoons brown sugar
1	teaspoon caraway seeds
	Freshly ground black pepper
3	tablespoons unsalted butter or canola oil
¼	cup unbleached all-purpose flour
2	cloves garlic, minced
	Salt to taste

Preheat the oven to 375°F.

For the vegetables and seitan, place the oil, onions, carrots, celery, and tamari in a heavy medium baking dish. Stir to coat the vegetables, then roast for 40 minutes. Remove the dish from the oven and place the seitan on top of the vegetables.

For the gravy, in a medium bowl, combine the stock, grape juice or wine, brown sugar, and caraway seeds, then pour over the seitan and vegetables. Season to taste with pepper, tightly cover the pan with aluminum foil, and return the pan to the oven. Bake for 40 minutes.

Remove the pan, uncover, and ladle out as much of the cooking broth as possible into a large liquid measuring cup. Heat butter or oil in a medium skillet over medium heat. Whisk in the flour and cook, whisking constantly, for 3 minutes. Slowly whisk in the reserved cooking broth and stir constantly until smooth and thick, 2 to 3 minutes. If you don't have enough broth left to make the gravy, add some more stock. Stir in half the garlic. Spread the gravy over the seitan, stirring to blend with any juices remaining in the pan. Add the salt to taste. For the glaze, change the oven setting to broil. In a small bowl, whisk together the grape juice or wine, brown sugar, miso paste, and the remaining garlic. Spoon the glaze over the seitan. Return the pan to the oven and broil, uncovered, until the gravy is bubbling hot and the seitan is deeply browned, about 5 minutes. Serve hot.

While brisket temperatures run low, emotions run high. Brisket lovers are incredibly opinionated. And not shy. While they might respect a brisket recipe that is not their own, that doesn't mean they won't question it. Or suggest ways to improve it. Or wonder why someone wouldn't do it their way to begin with. The problem is that while some things about brisket are factual and actual ("Collagen does not begin to break down at a significant rate until at least 160°F"), some are a *cri de coeur* ("I'm plotzing here. Ketchup? Cans of soup? OY!!" says a shocked visitor to a Chowhound brisket recipe discussion.) And natural areas of contention form around differences in saucing, serving, smoking, sides, and lots of other "s" words.

Major/minor disagreements aside, the brisket maker has a good heart (well, except for those who frequent the Midway at the Indiana State Fair). Nine times out of ten, he or she will try a taste of someone else's brisket and pretend to like wizened prunes or powdered mace.

Originally eaten only by the kitchen staff, brisket burnt ends are now a delicacy on the menu at most barbecue places.

50 Things About Brisket That People Can Disagree About

BRAISED BRISKET

1. How thick to slice it
2. How thin to slice it
3. When to slice it
4. What to cut it with
5. Electric Knife?
6. Serrated knife?
7. 4 lbs will serve 6–8
8. 4 lbs will serve 8–10
9. Always freeze
10. Never freeze
11. Go for the Le Creuset
12. Use any Dutch Oven with a tight seal
13. Serve at once
14. Serve the next day
15. Make it sweet
16. Make it savory
17. Brown it
18. Only brown it if you want to
19. Trim the fat before you cook
20. Leave on all the fat; it'll go into the meat
21. Trim fat to ¼"
22. Which cut? The point? The flat? Both? Neither?
23. Cryovac package
24. Never in a Cryovac

CORNED BEEF

25. Gray corned beef
26. Pink corned beef

BARBECUED BRISKET

27. Liquid Smoke
28. No Liquid Smoke
29. Best brand of Liquid Smoke
30. Weber
31. Big Green Egg
32. Texas Post Oak? Hickory? Red Oak?
33. Too much seasoning (can't taste the meat)
34. Needs seasoning
35. Start with the fat side up
36. Start with the fat side down
37. Slice thin (KC style)
38. Slice thick (TX style)

BRAISED AND BARBECUED

39. Seal in foil
40. No foil
41. Grass fed; corn fed, grass fed; grain-finished, feedlot
42. Some packaged ingredients okay
43. All packaged ingredients okay
44. No packaged ingredients ever
45. Recipe
46. Instinct
47. Measure precisely
48. A little of this, a little of that
49. Calling your recipe "the best ever" —pride?
50. Calling your recipe "the best ever?" —you from New York?

Zak Pelaccio in a rare moment of non-barbecue contemplation.

He'll tolerate the rookie who douses a brisket with Liquid Smoke and the non-purist who concocts a brisket entirely from things out of cans and jars and bottles. But I think it is safe to say that while a true brisketeer may countenance contradiction or lack of tradition, he or she will never put up with someone who is complacent about brisket making: a cook unable to accept constructive criticism or unwilling to raise the bar.

I had a conversation that bears this out with Fatty 'Cue Chef/Owner Zak Pelaccio, who is currently stunning palates with his barbecue fusion cuisine at Brooklyn restaurant Fatty 'Cue. Fatty 'Cue's brisket on bao sandwich was named by *New York Magazine* as the #1 sandwich in New York in 2009. Having tasted it, I think it is probably the #1 sandwich in the galaxy.

ME: "I know that you are constantly experimenting with your barbecue; asking, 'What if . . .,' trying new techniques, rethinking ingredients and flavor combinations. Do you have a goal?"

ZAK: "Yeah. That it's really fucking good."

ME: "Oh."

This is not to say that the brisket lover doesn't occasionally lighten up. Usually over a warm brisket sandwich and a cold beer. Listening to what could be the brisket national anthem, "The Way We Were," sung by Barbra Streisand: "I remember the time I knew what happiness was . . ." Even Proust didn't have a song. Perhaps this is the occasion to have brisket tell a joke or two and show its fun side.

The Last Brisket: A Joke

Courtesy of David Minkoff

Abie lay in his bed contemplating his impending death. Suddenly smelling the aroma of brisket, his favorite food, wafting up the stairs, he gathers his remaining strength and lifts himself from the bed. Leaning against the wall, he slowly makes his way out of the bedroom, and with even greater effort, gripping the railing with both hands he crawls downstairs.

With labored breath, he leans against the door frame and gazes into the kitchen. Were it not for death's agony, he would have thought himself already in Heaven. For there, on the kitchen table, was the biggest brisket he had ever seen.

He couldn't help thinking, was this already Heaven or was it one final act of love from his devoted wife of sixty-five years, Bessie, allowing him to leave this world a happy man?

With one great final effort, he throws himself toward the table, landing on his knees in a crumpled posture. His parched lips parted, the wondrous taste of the succulent meat already in his mouth seemingly brings him back to life. His aged and withered hand trembles as it grasps a carving knife laying next to the platter when it is suddenly smacked with a spatula by his wife.

"Don't touch that, Abie!" she shouts.

"That's for the shivah!"

The last laugh comes from Texas writer, historian, and barbecue expert Robb Walsh. When I told him that I had been searching in vain for a barbecued brisket joke, he offered me this: "Texans think putting 'New York' and 'barbecue' in the same sentence is a joke. What ya'll do to brisket is more like a crime." He added, "You can quote me." Maybe it's funnier if you don't live in New York.

ARRIVING AT ELLIS ISLAND   5202-1

2 The Amazing Adventures of Brisket

"The language of food, like any expressive medium, is never fixed, but perpetually a work in progress."

—Historian Jane Ziegelman

Avocados are from southern Mexico. Asian carp are from China. Goldfish (a very distant relative of carp) are from China and from Pepperidge Farm. Cashews come from equatorial South America; fennel from the Mediterranean. But where is brisket from? The best answers are: everywhere; all over the world; it depends on whom you ask. The best dialogue about this is one I had with food historian and founder of New York's Kitchen Arts & Letters, the very wise Nach Waxman.

ME: "Is there one original recipe for brisket?"

NACH WAXMAN: "It's like looking for the original recipe for toast. No one invented a brisket except a cow."

Not one to take "a cow" as an answer and already knowing that brisket has worldwide roots, I decided to try to re-create the brisket family tree. Which, it turns out, is tall, healthy, and still growing in many directions. The three different ways of cooking brisket help to explain its roots and its growth. While equally appreciated, braised brisket and barbecued brisket have two very different histories. Corned beef has a third. In the next chapter, you'll see that the cow (actually a steer) that invented brisket has its own story.

PART ONE: Braised Brisket. The Globe Trotter

"In praise of the braise. I was raised on brisket."

—*David Tanis*, A Platter of Figs

If you understand Jewish history and culture, you understand brisket. And if you understand brisket, you understand Jewish history and culture. While tradition and ritual define all Jewish food, three things defined brisket in America during the huge wave of immigration of the mid- to late-nineteenth century: Jewish dietary laws, memories, and economic imperatives. Kosher dietary laws, over 3,000 years old, were faithfully followed in America by most newly arrived Jewish homemakers, who were eager to maintain the customs they learned from their mothers. The biblical laws they followed said that only certain animals—those with cloven hooves and who chew their cud—were considered edible for a Jew. And only certain parts of that particular animal were permissible: for beef, only the forequarters could be eaten. Hence the ascendancy of the breast meat. So while many cuts of beef were taboo (sirloin, filet mignon, porterhouse) brisket was acceptable.

Food is "a part of and a window to who a community is, how that community came to be, how it exists at a particular moment in time, and what it values in the present and hopes for in the future," writes food historian Gil Marks in the *Encyclopedia of Jewish Food*. Marks could just as accurately have written that *brisket* is a part of and a window into a community. The warm memories of a food like brisket provided physical and emotional sustenance and gave it its powerful resonance once European immigrants reached Ellis Island.

Back in their hometowns in Germany or Russia or Austria, the cooking techniques and ingredients might have varied, but brisket was traditionally served as a Sabbath dish or as a celebratory meal for a holiday like Chanukah. If brisket originally spoke of family and community, it still does. To that point, brisket will never be a meal for one. It doesn't come in a single-serving size in the freezer of a supermarket. While Lean Cuisine offers eleven varieties in its Comfort Cuisine line, there's no brisket. Whoever first said "Share the love" (Jerry Garcia?) must have been referring to a gentle, meltingly tender home-cooked brisket, at once filling and fulfilling.

Economics has always played a part in who eats it, who doesn't, and why someone would choose Oysters Rockefeller instead. Brisket—boiled, stewed, simmered, braised—came to this country with European Jewish immigrants affluent enough to have served it back home. While brisket was an inexpensive cut in Europe, it was still prohibitively expensive for most newly arrived immigrant cooks in America. Gil Marks astutely observes that brisket has come full circle. It started as a rare indulgence and is a rare indulgence again today, for two reasons: today's rising prices (like skirt steak and flat iron, the cut is much more in demand; prices vary—and so does quality—but brisket today can go from a sale price of around $3 a pound at a supermarket to $89.98 for a USDA Prime nine-pound whole beef brisket at a top New York butcher very near where Bernie Madoff lived) and the fact that rich fat-marbled red meat is now anathema to pretty much everyone except for a devout Atkins dieter. With endearing ingenuousness, writer Joanna G. Harris, in a recent online review of new Jewish cookbooks, notes: "I don't know the medical facts, but pastrami

Katz's deli, founded by Russian immigrants in 1888 and still going strong.

A classic brisket from Cook's Illustrated. Fork-tender, accompanied by gossamer mashed potatoes. Recipe p.158.

sandwiches and cheesecake, combined with big cigars and a sedentary life at the pinochle table, are said to produce heart attacks." Oh. Really?

The first Jewish recipes for brisket in America were the familiar ones passed down from mothers and grandmothers. And they were primarily from Ashkenazi Jews, whose roots were in Germany. "Ashkenazic brisket," says Gil Marks, "is always made with onions and plenty of them. After the mid-nineteenth century, potatoes and carrots were frequently added to provide more sustenance." What these recipes lacked in creativity, they made up for in familiar satisfaction and bulk. Ashkenazic food habits ultimately became known as "typical Jewish food."

Here, I would like to take a moment to point out that brisket is both remarkably notable and endlessly quotable. It is amazing how much history a steer breast has. Certainly much more than my own illustrious Russian/Swedish family, never much heralded outside of Moscow, Göteburg, or Baltimore. And my family only traveled to places like Maine; New Jersey; Rehoboth Beach, Delaware; and Atlantic City.

James Beard, in his book *James Beard's American Cookery*, notes that "10 million immigrants came to this country between 1830 and 1880." He talks about the influence of French immigrants in New England whose traditions had taught them how to slow cook and tenderize beef; German immigrants in Pennsylvania who moved to the Middle West with their vinegar-marinated roasts; and the introduction of French-inspired beef daubes to Southern cities like New Orleans. While it seems that no brisket recipe—Jewish or non-Jewish—appeared in any cookbook earlier than 1899, historians say that the meat would have been cooked—in an urban immigrant community like the Lower East Side in New York—over an open hearth or in a community stove, with only onions, water, and perhaps a few peppercorns for flavor. Or it could have been a stew, made more cheaply with only pieces of brisket. As economic fortunes rose, so did the popularity of brisket. By the early twentieth century, a whole new group of immigrant Jews became able to afford it. Delis and restaurants opened in cities, so brisket became available outside the home. And it had social status: eating as much meat as you wanted was one way of showing how rich you were. Brisket's popularity also went up because it was a food that could be easily Americanized and updated. "The language of food, like any expressive medium, is never fixed, but perpetually a work in progress," observes historian Jane Ziegelman, author of *97 Orchard: An Edible History of Five Immigrant Families in One New York Tenement*. As Jews moved around the country, their recipes started to take on local flavors. In New England, cider replaced water; chiles found their way into briskets in New Mexico.

Yet a central conflict remained. Jewish immigrants struggled to balance their desire to honor traditions with their desire to assimilate. Umlauts were dropped. Last names were anglicized. Sauerbraten recipes lost their lebkuchen. As time went on, fewer women kept kosher homes. The opportunities to taste the offerings of their new country were too tempting to pass up. Even rabbis supported this: food historian and Jewish cookbook author Joan Nathan recounts the story of the beginning of the liberal Reform movement in America. Its leader, Rabbi Isaac Meyer Wise, called for widespread changes. One was to liberalize dietary laws to the point where, at an eight-course banquet in Cincinnati in 1883, celebrating the graduation of the first class of American Reform rabbis, non-kosher dishes like littleneck clams, shrimp, soft-shell crabs, and frog's legs with cream were paraded out to the shocked guests. Jews' eagerness to embrace a different lifestyle and Americanize themselves is consistent with all of Jewish history. Centuries of global religious persecution meant that Jews have always been on the move. Jane Ziegelman notes that "where most cuisines are moored to a place, Jewish cooking transcends geography." It is not surprising, she adds, that Jews have always been "among the world's most avid culinary borrowers." So whether they came to America from France or Germany or were descendants of Jews from North Africa or Syria or China, they had a natural willingness to combine the old with the new.

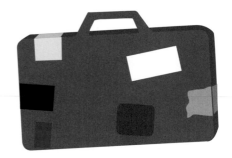

Fast-forward to how Jewish cooks transformed brisket recipes and how American innovations transformed Jewish cooks. Joan Nathan points out that as American technology goes, so goes the brisket. A few early examples come from her book *Jewish Cooking in America*: "Coal and wood-burning stoves replaced open hearths; refrigerators replaced endless salting, smoking, and preserving." By the turn of the twentieth century, new commercial products were flowing onto the market. Hence, for the first time, such prepared foods as slices of cranberry sauce, cups of ketchup and chili sauce, and condensed mushroom soup went into briskets. Non-kosher cooks appreciated the ease of shortcuts and new tastes. It didn't take long for companies like Maxwell House and Heinz to realize what a large and eager market they would have if these products had rabbinical approval: in 1923, Heinz Vegetarian Baked Beans became the first kosher American brand of food. In 1935, Coca-Cola was declared kosher.

"I think the rule of thumb might be that a brisket can't be from the Old World if it is made with Diet Dr Pepper in the New World."

Brisket gained new bedfellows. And it gained new fans. "Thanks to the canning industry, every type of essential food from soup to nuts is available in neat cans or glass containers," enthuses Jewish cookbook writer Leah W. Leonard in her 1949 book, *Jewish Cookery*. She goes on to suggest that there should be a special emergency shelf in every home for help with "last minute meals." What "emergency" would force "the handy homemaker" to spring into action in Ms. Leonard's opinion? "That occasion may be when unexpected guests stay to luncheon or dinner, or when weather conditions unavoidably postpone a trip to the grocery, meat market, or delicatessen shop. Or when illness of the kitchen engineer makes emergency meals necessary." ("Kitchen engineer!" Yes, you! And you don't even have to go to engineering school!)

These newfangled ingredients may be kosher—Lipton Ranch Soup Mix, podner?—but what, exactly, is a Jewish food? Gil Marks believes that "a Jewish food is one that is almost sanctified, either by its repeated use or use within the holidays or rituals." Like, say . . . brisket. Joan Nathan is of the opinion that because Jews "have lived in so many places, there is no 'Jewish' food other than matzah, haroset (the Passover spread); or cholent or chamim (the Sabbath stews that surface in different forms in every land where Jews have lived." Which were sometimes made with . . . that's right . . . brisket.

What better match for this versatile, can-do, "go ahead and put in the mango chutney!" dish than America, the land of brisket opportunity? Here's to life, liberty, and the pursuit of kosher Coca-Cola Cherry Zero.

What did Ashkenazic, Sephardic, and Mizrachi Jews eat? Hint: location, location, location. There are several subgroups of Jews, each with a distinct culinary tradition. Etymology begins to explain their geography. The word *Ashkenazic* is derived from the Hebrew word for Germany. *Sephardic* is derived from the Hebrew word for Spain. *Mizrachi* is from the Hebrew word for Eastern.

Ashkenazi Jews came from Germany, Austria, Romania, Poland, the Baltic countries, Russia, and parts of France. They lived in colder regions, so it's not surprising that their foods tended to be hearty and substantial. Based on what was available seasonally and on local specialties, meat, fish, black breads, potatoes, potato dumplings, root vegetables, savory stews, and soups were popular. So were sweet-

Why Braised Brisket is a Cold-Weather Dish

Well, first of all, because you're much more likely to say, "I'll have the Caesar Salad" than you are "I'll have the heavy, high-cal, put-some-meat-on-my bones brisket with the gravy-rich potatoes." Nor is brisket the go-to food when you're thinking, "I've got three months to rock this bikini." "Light, cool, refreshing" are not among its considerable attributes.

But, historically, in pre-bikini times, there is another explanation for when brisket is eaten and it, too, is seasonal. Historian of all foods Jewish, Gil Marks, points out that "in the summer, animals could graze and eat free; come winter, these animals were not going to breed or work—plus they had to be fed. So they were slaughtered around Chanukah." Thus brisket became a traditional winter holiday dish. Marks adds, "Once again, necessity proved the Jewish mother's source of invention."

and-sour dishes like borscht and meat and vegetable stews. Theirs was not a cuisine of delicate herbs and spices.

Sephardic Jews came from Spain, Portugal, North Africa, and the Middle East. Joyce Goldstein, in her book, *Sephardic Flavors: Jewish Cooking of the Mediterranean,* discusses the foods of Spain and Portugal and the adaptations Jews made as they moved into the Ottoman Empire. Theirs was an aromatic sunny cuisine that favored sweet-and-sour dishes, tart sauces, and vinaigrettes. Sephardic cuisine is light in character. Fresh lemon juice was added to sauces and soups. There were salads, stuffed vegetables, vine leaves, olive oil, fruits, herbs, nuts, and chickpeas.

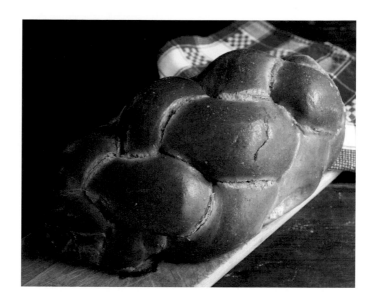

"A Jewish food is one that is almost sanctified, either by its repeated use or use within the holidays or rituals."

—Gil Marks

Mizrachi Jews were descendants of Jews from the Middle East, Central Asia, and the Caucasus. Other subgroups are Yemenite, Ethiopian, and Asian; their cuisine reflects their wide diversity. A Sabbath dinner would include meat dishes, usually lamb or beef. Everyday meals would feature vegetables—cooked, stuffed, and baked. Beans, chickpeas, lentils, bulgur, and rice replaced potatoes; flatbreads replaced challah. Fresh ingredients, dried fruits, and savory spices were features of their cuisine.

PART TWO: Barbecued Brisket

"When my life is through, bury me in barbeque."

—"The BBQ Song," Rhett & Link & The Homestead Pickers

If there are two things you should know about barbecuing brisket it's that "low and slow" is the cooking mantra and that, of all the meats you can barbecue, brisket is the hardest one to get right. "Even when you follow all the recipe instructions to the letter, brisket often comes out dry . . . It's hard to mess up a pork roast, but it's easy to ruin a brisket," says Texas barbecue authority and author Robb Walsh in his book, *Legends of Texas Barbecue Cook Book: Recipes and Recollections from the Pit Bosses.*

"Patience" is what every single barbecue veteran will counsel you. (Or maybe they just tell me that because I'm from New York and have very little of it.) An ardent barbecue fan writes online: "The good Lord intended brisket to be smoked slowly, and this requires the deepest of all passions. More passion is required of me to smoke a brisket than I have for flying AH-64D Longbow Apaches, and that is saying a whole lot." Amen. But it is worth it. If braised brisket fans are zealots, barbecue cooks and chroniclers are total maniacs. They present opinions as facts. "As barbecue is one of the few aliments that unaccountably don't trigger our bodies' built-in satiation response, it is impossible to stop eating barbecue once you get started," says food writer Jeffrey Steingarten in his introduction to *Peace, Love, and Barbecue* by Mike Mills and Amy Mills Tunnicliffe. Barbecue devotees don't just have history: they have lore and legends. They don't have stories, they have tall tales and mythology. And that terrific song from Louis Armstrong. What are the origins of barbecue—and barbecued brisket—in America? Well, not surprisingly there are many conflicting theories. Of course. (To get it straight, "barbecue" is the technique of long, slow, steady smoking off heat; putting hamburgers on the grill over direct heat is "grilling," not "barbecuing.") While braised brisket pretty much came over in steerage, barbecue, or at least roasted meat, has a more illustrious heritage. It has been suggested that both Thomas Jefferson and George Washington included references to barbecue in their writings, referring, most likely, to the pig roasts that were traditional in England. But that's the end of the fancy pedigree.

Everything at Slows in Detroit is warm and welcoming, including the brisket:
Niman Ranch-sourced, "dry rubbed and smoked heavy . . . "

Jeffrey Steingarten *thinks* cooking meat in a smoky pit probably originated in the Caribbean. (Others suggest South America.) Slaves, who came to America from these locales, brought with them their simple but revolutionary barbecue techniques. And it was in America's Deep South where their innovative cooking skills were first noticed and appreciated. Some historians say that barbecue was then introduced outside of the South by African Americans who left that region and moved to other parts of the country looking for work.

What was barbecued was a matter of taste and availability: the meat could be pork, lamb, chicken, or beef. Lines were drawn. Through much of the southeastern United States, pork was—and still is—the star of the show: chopped, sliced, or pulled and served on buns. Barbecue expert Ardie Davis, who is from Kansas City and who keeps an open mind, told me, "People who think that pork is the one true barbecue meat . . . well, I call them 'hogmatic.'"

In Texas and much of the western United States, beef brisket rules. One of my new favorite events is the Fourth of July "Texas Brew-B-Que." The online flyer for it enthuses, "Texans know it's all about the Beer and the Bar-B-Que! Add a Brisket Cook-Off Competition with 5,000 lbs FREE BRISKET, live music and you have one heck of a party!" Could it get any better? You bet! Ready? Fireworks! Beer pong! Chihuahua races!

In Arkansas, Oklahoma, Kansas, and Missouri, where the southeastern and southwestern traditions merge, beef and pork are equally popular. In Chicago and other cities where African Americans settled, pork ribs are on the menu, rather than whole hogs or pork shoulders. What is called the "barbecue belt" runs all the mouthwatering way from North Carolina to Texas. This most local of all delicacies, "Barbecue varies county by county within a single state," says John T. Edge, a great eater, a great writer, and the director of the Southern Foodways Alliance.

"Compared to other parts of this country, New York isn't exactly a barbecue destination," understates Serious Eats. But it does have its own urban spin and you can take the subway from Harlem to Williamsburg to Midtown to find it. Local or express to Blue Smoke's regional barbecue styles from across the country to Texas-style barbecue at Hill Country to Mile End's Montreal cured and smoked meats to Dinosaur's jam-packed, juicy and sassy Southern flavors.

Love me tender. The ultimate barbecue slogan and promise from House Park Bar-B-Que in Austin, Texas.

There are homegrown competitive barbecue champions like Clint Cantwell from Garden City, Long Island, captain of Smoke in Da Eye BBQ Team. And only in New York would you find a brisket sandwich where the meat comes from California, the cheese comes from Vermont, the buns come from Chinatown, and the pit master comes from Queens. As much a melting pot as a smoker, the sandwich is the pride of Fatty 'Cue's late-night menu.

Like braised brisket, barbecued brisket's fortunes were impacted by geography and economics. Central Texas—where brisket is king—has barbecue traditions that evolved from a confluence of events in the second half of the nineteenth century. Refugees from the Civil War came to Texas looking for new land and a new start, bringing along their recipes and cooking styles. Around the same time, German and Czech butchers—recent immigrants from Europe—introduced their practice of slowly smoking meat. Huge herds of cattle traveled on The Chisholm Trail, so there was an abundance of beef. As Kelly Alexander wrote in *Saveur*, "Cow hunters would round up free-roaming cattle and while the hindquarters went for a lot of money, the tougher forequarters (brisket among them) went for very little." Immigrants from Eastern Europe would smoke them "the Old World way, over a wood fire, for their own version of brisket." Explains Gil Marks, "Among non-Jews in America, brisket was for a long time a disregarded cut of meat, practically given away or used for ground beef. Except in Texas. In Texas, bbq means succulent brisket."

More than braised brisket or corned beef, barbecued brisket comes with wacky names and snappy sayings: "Need no teef to eat my beef," from Austin, Texas' House Park Bar-B-Que. "At least the salt is kosher" is the tagline for a team of Jewish 'cue competitors. "Put your lips on a hot chick," suggests a poster advertising the Jack Daniels World Championship Invitational Barbecue. And who wouldn't want to go a festival called "The Big Pig Jig" or root (no pun intended) for a team called "Here for the Beer."

Found in Translation

When you want to order it in Maestricht or Majorca or Milan, brisket translations:

Dansk (Danish)
n. - bryststykke

Nederlands (Dutch)
borststuk (vlees)

Français (French)
n. - (Culin) poitrine

Deutsch (German)
n. - Bruststück

Ελληνική (Greek)
**n. - ακρόστερνο, πρόσθια
στερνική χώρα, (μαγειρ.)
στήθος**

Italiano (Italian)
punta di petto di bovino

Português (Portuguese)
**n. - carne (f) do peito de um
animal**

Русский (Russian)
грудинка

Español (Spanish)
**n. - carne cortada del
pecho de un animal**

Svenska (Swedish)
n. - bringa

中文（简体）(Chinese (Simplified))
胸部, 胸肉

中文（繁體）(Chinese (Traditional))
n. - 胸部, 胸肉

한국어 (Korean)
n. - 동물의 가슴

日本語 (Japanese)
n. - 胸部, 胸肉

العربية (Arabic)
‏(اللحم) محل صدر البقرة‏

עברית (Hebrew)
n. - ‏דד, עטין‏

동물의 가슴

Pour it on!

"I've got 52 sauces. Different flavors. I started with just a regular, then I did hot, then mild. Now I got an international sauce, from the islands, and a spicy sour sauce. Those are all I want to tell you about. I also have 52 coleslaws."

—*Kansas City barbecue legend Grace Harris, saveur.com*

Life is rosy, and so is this colorful corned beef.

PART THREE: Corned Beef

The origins of corned beef and cabbage are a little murky. Even its legitimacy as a true Irish dish is in dispute. There's no real consensus on how it got to America. Or how to cook it. Or even whether you should bother when it takes forever and you can so easily buy it. Corned beef is brined beef, usually brisket. The brine is some combination of water, salt, and pickling spices, and the process can take up to three weeks. The term *corned* has nothing to do with the brisket being made with corn. Instead, it's believed to come from the fact that the meat had originally been dry cured with coarse salt to preserve it, back before refrigeration, and it was observed that the grains of the salt were about the same size as corn kernels. Hence *corned.* There *is* consensus that only in New England do corned beef eaters like their corned beef gray. (Add sodium nitrate to turn it a rosy pink.) On corned beef getting its pink color from nitrates: if that sounds scary, a prominent food scientist told me "Nitrates fix the pigment (myloglobin). And it's a natural pigment."

GRAY CORNED BEEF   PINK CORNED BEEF

Historian Jane Ziegelman, in her very comprehensive book, believes that "though corned beef and cabbage traveled to the United States with the first Dutch settlers in the early seventeenth century, many of the groups that followed, including the English, the Germans, and the Jews, emigrated with their own corned beef traditions." She says that while corned beef and cabbage were thought to have been on every immigrant Irishman's plate, "many of the poor Irish who arrived in the United States after the 1840s had likely never even tasted it." Others say that bacon and cabbage was the real Irish tradition, not corned beef and cabbage. Of course they don't mean the skinny bacon strips we have today, but a gutsier kind of cured pork. One Irish-American blogger suggests that "Irish immigrants to America were introduced to corned beef by their Jewish neighbors, and those who could not afford the more costly bacon substituted it, eventually forming a new tradition." Or perhaps corned beef and cabbage became popular in America at Irish pubs. In her book *The Festive Foods of Ireland*, author Darina Allen, who runs the Ballymaloe Cooking School in County Cork, says, "Although this dish is rarely eaten nowadays in Ireland, for Irish-Americans it conjures up powerful nostalgic images of a rural Irish past."

Colman Andrews, writing in his James Beard Award-winning book *The Country Cooking of Ireland*, says: "The fact is that corned beef has been eaten, with and without cabbage, in Ireland since at least the 1600s. Under the name 'salt beef' it was exported in large quantities from Cork to continental Europe, the West Indies, and Newfoundland." Andrews is well aware that Irish "experts" delight in saying that corned beef and cabbage is a combination Irish immigrants developed only because they couldn't find the bacon for their beloved bacon and cabbage. But he told me that it's almost impossible to believe that cured pork loin wasn't available in places like New York or Cleveland where there were sizable immigrant populations. Why so much misinformation, I asked him? He believes that going viral with information isn't just an online phenomenon. All it takes is for one person to say it or print it and it gets passed on as fact. Before the Internet, going viral just took longer!

But the last word goes to Francis Lam, himself a first-generation American of Chinese descent. Lam, a senior writer at salon.com, talks about how much people really care about Irish traditions. In a charming and erudite piece, "St. Patrick's Day Controversy: Is Corned Beef and Cabbage Irish?", he reveals that in the third grade, he took the Irishness of it all seriously enough to start referring to himself as "Francis McLam" as St. Patrick's Day approached. So, the grown-up Mr. Lam investigates the origins of corned beef and cabbage—on the Salon site with his readers, food historians, cultural experts, cookbook writers, Irish Americans, and Irish Irish. And like so many other "native" dishes that somehow got to America and stuck around, he basically concludes: Who cares? "Each of the experts I spoke to would agree on one thing: that there isn't really a point in arguing about authenticity, because authenticity always changes. People make up traditions all the time, so why is it that only traditions old enough for you to forget how they got made up in the first place are the 'real' ones?"

"Corned beef looks like an uncle of yours that's been on the beach for way too long..."

—*Novelist Gary Shteyngart in an interview with* Gigantic *magazine*

Brisket Etymology. Or Should It Be "Eat-ymology"?

After having done my own due diligence researching the origins of the word brisket, I struck gold and found Professor Anatoly Liberman, author of Word Origins . . . and How We Know Them. *He blew me away with his very learned explanation leavened by a great sense of humor. I first e-mailed him on his etymology site blog.us@oup.com, where he encourages queries, never thinking that he would acknowledge, let alone answer my question about the origins of the word* brisket. *Let alone place this treasure trove on his site just a week or so later. I am giving this to you in its glorious entirety.*

From "Breast" to "Brisket"

By Anatoly Liberman

It seems reasonable that brisket should in some way be related to breast: after all, brisket is the breast of an animal. But the path leading from one word to the other is neither straight nor narrow. Most probably, it does not even exist. In what follows I am greatly indebted to the Swedish scholar Bertil Sandahl, who published an article on brisket and its cognates in 1964. The Oxford English Dictionary has no citations of brisket prior to 1450, but Sandahl discovered bresket in a document written in 1328-1329, and if his interpretation is correct, the date should be pushed back quite considerably. Before 1535, the favored (possibly, the only) form in English was bruchet(te).

The English word is surrounded with many look-alikes from several languages: Middle French bruchet, brichet, brechet (Modern French bréchet ~ brechet "breastbone"; in French dialects, one often finds -q- instead of -ch-), Breton bruch ~ brusk ~ bresk "breast (of a horse)," along with bruched "breast," Modern Welsh brysced (later brwysged ~ brysged), and Irish Gaelic brisgein "cartilage (as of the nose)." Then there are German Bries ~ Briesel ~ Brieschen ~ Bröschen "the breast gland of a calf," Old Norse brjósk "cartilage, gristle," and several words from the modern Scandinavian languages for "sweetbread" (Swedish bräs, Norwegian bris, and Danish brissel), which, as it seems, belong here too (sweetbread is, of course, not bread: it is the pancreas or thymus, especially of a calf, used as food; bread in sweetbread is believed to go back to an old word for "flesh"). Many words for "breast" in the languages of the world begin with the grating sound groups br- ~ gr- ~ -khr-, as though to remind us of our breakable, brittle, fragile bones (fraction, fragile, and fragment, all going back to the same Latin root, once began with bhr).

At first blush, brisket, with its pseudo-diminutive suffix, looks like a borrowing from French. But there is a good rule: a word is native in a language in which it has recognizable cognates. To be sure, sometimes no cognates are to be seen or good candidates present . . . themselves in more languages than one, but etymology is not an exact science, and researchers should be thankful for even approximate signposts along the way. In French, bréchet is isolated (and nothing similar has been found in other Romance languages), while in Germanic, brjósk, bris, bräs, and others (see them above) suggest kinship with brisket. Therefore, the opinion prevails that brisket is of Germanic origin. Émile Littré, the author of a great, perennially useful French dictionary, thought that the French word had been borrowed from English during the Hundred Year War (1337–1453), and most modern etymologists tend to agree with him. Then the Celtic words would also be from English (for they too are isolated in their languages), and the etymon of brisket would be either Low (that is, northern) German bröske "sweetbread" or Old Norse brjósk, allied to Old Engl. breosan "break." The original meaning of brisket may have been "something (easily breakable?) in the breast of a (young?) animal." If so, contrary to expectation, brisket is not related to breast, for breast appears to have been coined with the sense "capable of swelling," rather than "capable of breaking" (see my earlier post on breast). Those who insist on the Celtic origin of brisket have a hard time making their case. Needless to say, brisk is not related to brisket.

The reconstruction given above (an English word that spread to French, Irish, and Welsh, an anatomical term designating a brittle part of the breast in an animal's body) is acceptable, but it leaves the suffix -et unaccounted for. Though rarely, -et does occur in native English words.

The best example is thicket, but in such cases it is usually possible to explain how the noun acquired such an unusual look. More often it seems that French -et was appended to native nouns, as probably happened in the history of hornet, tippet, and strumpet. Brisket could be part of that group (the simplest conjecture). Sandahl offered a most ingenious hypothesis. Middle English had the word ket "meat," taken over from Scandinavian, and Sandahl suggested that perhaps there was a compound like brusk-ket or brust-ket "a piece of gristly flesh." Such a compound may indeed have existed, but we have no way of ascertaining its presence and for the time being will stay with the suffix -et. Thus, it appears that brisket is a Germanic word of Low German or Scandinavian descent embellished with a French suffix, in order to make the dish more palatable: originally, brösk-et or brjósk-et. (In similar fashion, -et turned a homey Germanic floozy into a classy French prostitute: from strump- to strumpet.) However, the earliest form we know is brushet(te). Its vowel may have been pronounced as ü and reflected an unfamiliar foreign sound, which later yielded brisket and occasionally bresket.

NOTE: This first appeared in the blog "Oxford Etymologist" on the Web site of Oxford University Press. It is reprinted here with Dr. Liberman's permission.

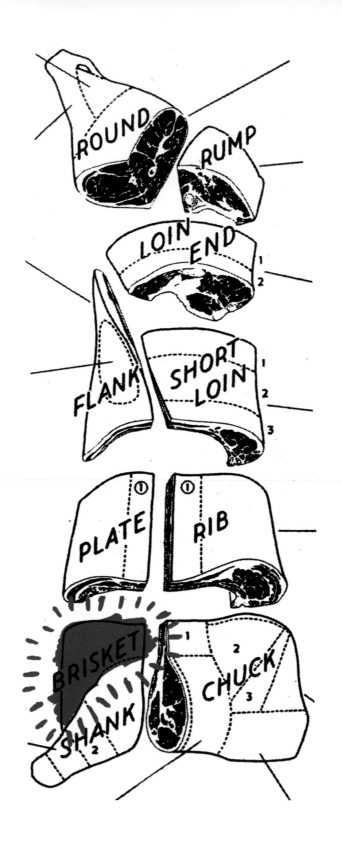

3 Meet the Cow. Meet the Meat. Meet the Butcher.

> "A vague beef-buyer is open to countless unnecessary disappointments and expenses . . ."
>
> —*Julia Child*

MEET THE COW

I think it took me longer to find out where brisket comes from than it did for me to find out where babies come from. In my quest for brisket knowledge, I had to find out about the animal itself. First I read that brisket comes from a cow. Then I read that it comes from a steer. Which is it? Both? Are these animals interchangeable? Do they get along?

Here's how Michael Pollan, the man who just socked it to everyone with his brilliant 2006 blockbuster, *The Omnivore's Dilemma*, answered me. "Cow technically is a grown-up female. Most meat, or at least primal cuts, come from steers." From the ALL-CAP school of explanations: "A steer is NEVER a cow. Never." That's what Nicolette Hahn Niman, co-owner of BN Ranch and the author of *Righteous Porkchop*, shot back ten minutes after I sent her an e-mail. Then I heard back from Texas barbecue expert Robb Walsh, who gave me an explanation that all Texans probably know from birth: "Steer is a neutered male. Our tender graded beef comes from young steers—we also slaughter older cows when they are done raising calves." He added, "A cow does have a brisket, of course, but it tends to be tougher than the steers and heifers slaughtered for meat." (A heifer, by the way, is a female who has not yet had a calf.) "The brisket recovered from slaughtered cows is generally used for processed meats, such as corned beef and pastrami."

Frankly, even though I now do understand that good brisket comes from young steers, sometimes it's easier to just refer to it as "the animal." As in, "this cut" comes from "that" part of "the animal." Or that "brisket" comes from the forequarters of the "beef." The fact that the animal on the cover of this book is batting its (not his or her) lashes, just embraces the Eddie Izzardness of it all and reinforces the gender-neutral notion that brisket welcomes diversity. Here's a terminology bonus for going through all this: The plural of beef is beeves. And a trivia bonus: Robb Walsh, explaining about what comes from where, adds, "And the meat from bulls is used in kosher hot dogs!" Oy.

But the first point (cow/steer/animal) is pretty much a non-issue compared to the second point. Which is: How is the animal raised? What was it fed? Why? Will the choices made make for more humanely raised animals, better beef, cheaper meat, better PR? Who gets to decide which practices are best? And what is "best"? Let me just cut to the chase. After months of investigating and learning and after listening to some really heated debates, it's clear that the people who raise the animals we eat will all pretty much say out loud that their very pc goal is delicious, natural, and affordable meat from humanely raised and slaughtered animals. But this is a murky arena, where words like "sustainable," "humanely raised," "natural," and "farm" can be thrown around like grenades and take on many different meanings. Beware, says Michael Pollan, of marketing terms like "health-conscious" farms that boast "organic beef" raised in "organic feedlots." Beware, I say, of applauding beef that's raised the "old-fashioned" way or a ranch that champions its "natural feeding practices," says it's "eco-friendly," or tells us that it embraces "green ag." It sounds good, but what does it mean?

"There's no way to write about eating meat these days without offending someone."
—Regina Schrambling, epicurious.com

It turns out that "organic" practices, when it comes to USDA beef, are open to a very liberal interpretation. So the term "grass-fed" is still waiting for a strict government codification. (The USDA is currently developing guidelines to define it as an animal-fed all-grass diet of at least 95 percent.) "Sustainable" is clearer and more quantitative. It means avoiding pesticides and fertilizer in an effort to help sustain the environment; not using hormones or antibiotics in order to sustain the quality of the beef; developing a caring community of people who will cook the meat and sell the meat in an effort to sustain a best-practices way of life. There is no government or independent oversight of "sustainable" beef, but on this too, there is progress on developing more formalized standards.

There's a lot that's fraught. And there is a lot in flux. For every argument, there's a counterargument. The zealots—passionate authors, outspoken food fanatics, vegan bloggers, pro-beef Web sites, artisanal butchers, and online foodies—seem clear enough to themselves, but it's confusing to the rest of us. We know what's bad (feedlots, factory farming, giving antibiotics to animals to keep them healthy, adding growth hormones and steroids to their diet, a word like commodity when it's next to beef) but we're not sure of what's really good. Or why.

Here's what you would do in the best of all possible worlds: make friends with an outstanding butcher or meat purveyor or even order meat from a respected supplier who sells online. All of these sources would help familiarize you with the highest standards and latest practices so you could make an informed, intelligent decision. And then there's the reality of standing in front of the meat counter at Stop & Shop, shopping for a brisket for Sunday dinner. You see the brisket wrapped like a mummy in Cryovac, encapsulating some bloody residue and looking anything but fresh, sustainable, or natural. You're thinking, "Oh, that can't be good. Can it?" Well . . . can it?

It can. Depending. Mostly yes. It is the industry standard. According to Tom Mylan, executive butcher and co-owner of the The Meat Hook in Brooklyn, New York, writing on The Atlantic Life site, "upwards of 90 percent of the beef taken home by American grocery store shoppers is in plastic-wrapped foam trays." But since a butcher (and many do) could take it out before he/she trims it and sells it to you, you might not be aware that your meat has been shipped vacuum sealed. Vacuum sealing has been around since the 1960s. What we get in this very tightly sealed, no-shrinkage, oxygen-free package is what most people call "wet aged"—beef that's aging in its own juices. The opposite—"dry aging"—means just that, exposing the meat to air and letting it age in a cool, controlled environment for as long as ten weeks. Costs more, tastes better, sounds cooler. Think four-star steak house.

So. Am I the only all-American brisketeer who still thinks that the blood inside the Cryovac package is kind of creepy? Of course not! That is why God made the Internet. There are the chat rooms where discerning meat buyers debate perceived negatives of the smell when you open the seal (from "slightly noticeable" to "ick" and "ugh") and raise questions about freshness. On ChefTalk, a site with forums for chefs and home cooks, you'll find the following topic: "Cryovac-wet-aged-beef-stinky." And an online acknowledgment, from Pulitzer prize—winning food critic Jonathan Gold, that some chefs love to "break down animals" so they can "explore all the delicious squishy bits that go missing when you get your meat in Cryovac-sealed parcels shipped from Iowa." Smack!

But when it comes to meat (well, when it comes to anything), no one is shy. I went to a brisket cooking class given by Manhattan butcher shop owner (a fifth-generation butcher) and brisket maven, Tony Schatzie. From the question-and-answer part of the class:

ME: "How would you feel about someone buying their brisket at, say, Costco?"

TONY: "The same way I feel about my wife going out with another man."

For another take, I turned to an expert with an unforgettable name: J. Kenji Lopez-Alt. Kenji, in his own words, is "the executive editor/recipe czar at Serious Eats," where he writes the totally smart "Food Lab" column. This is a man who brings science, analytical thinking, a well-educated palate, and a cheerful real-world sensibility to everything he looks at. Not to mention an engineering degree from MIT and serious chef cred. Since I had been getting such different answers about vacuum sealing and aging meat, I begged Kenzi to tell me what he thought and raised my concerns about vacuum sealing. Here's what he told me:

"I don't think there's anything wrong with Cryovac. Most of the beef you buy in supermarkets or even butchers these days is delivered in large Cryovac-ed cuts that are then broken down and packaged for sale. So even if you see raw brisket out on the butcher's counter, chances are it came as a whole (point and flat attached together) Cryovac-ed cut that the butcher then repackaged for sale.

"You hear talk about 'wet aging' often, which is really just a euphemism for 'Cryovac-ed and shipped.' Basically, the meat sits in its Cryovac bag for a few weeks, and during that time, some enzymatic breakdown of muscle and connective tissue occurs that can tenderize it to a degree, though the flavor doesn't develop the way it does with dry-aged beef. This can be important and a good thing for cuts that you're going to cook as a steak. For long-cooking cuts like brisket, it doesn't make much difference, since you cook it long enough to break down all that tissue anyway.

"So," he says, "the point is, Cryovac-ed brisket is fine to buy, neither better nor worse than non-Cryovac-ed stuff (which was most likely Cryovac-ed at some point anyway). You might end up paying a little more per pound for that actual meat since the Cryovac bag retains

Slabs of grass-fed brisket in the process of being broken down at Marlow & Daughers.

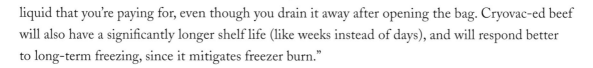

"What else can you do with the cut? You can make corned beef or pastrami. But let me tell you, there are corned beefs and pastramis that should have stayed briskets."

—*Robbie Richter, Pit Master, Fatty 'Cue*

liquid that you're paying for, even though you drain it away after opening the bag. Cryovac-ed beef will also have a significantly longer shelf life (like weeks instead of days), and will respond better to long-term freezing, since it mitigates freezer burn."

Kenji also mentioned that he thinks the blood is kind of creepy too. But my verdict is: get over it. Get on with it. Unless you are at a "boutique butcher," vacuum sealed is how brisket is sold today and it will be good. Just not OMG great. But how many people get to go to a butcher who is breaking down fresh-killed meat every week or shop on a daily basis at a local farmers' market? Not I.

If aging and packaging are minor skirmishes, how the animal is fed and raised is the war. Basically, there are three types of practices today:

- Animals can be entirely corn fed.
- Animals can be grass fed, grain (corn) finished.
- Animals can be entirely grass fed.

One of the problems is that most of the individuals who weigh in on this truly believe that one particular methodology is the only way to raise cattle. Of course it's *their* way. It is incredibly refreshing to talk to someone like Nicolette Hahn Niman, who dares to suggest that there are a number of viable ways to raise beef and more than one acceptable choice for a consumer. She is also candid about the fact that enlightened ranchers are always re-examining existing practices and trying new ones. "We [she and her rancher husband] are now doing all grass fed," she says. "But we did do grass fed, grain finished at Niman Ranch—because chefs wanted more fat on the animals."

It really comes down to this: Is it good for the planet? Good for the animal? Good for the brisket eater? Does it taste good? And how does economics fit in?

We know Mr. Pollan's brilliantly articulated grass-fed vs. corn-fed manifesto. In brief, most cattle today are corn fed. But corn is an unnatural and unhealthy diet because the animal is an herbivore. What comes naturally is grazing in a pasture and feeding on grass. Which is what cattle used to do. Animals were first fed a corn diet because corn was cheap and plentiful. It fattened them up and helped marbleize their flesh; they could be slaughtered and processed at an earlier age and therefore turn more of a profit. (Cows raised on all grass take longer to reach their optimum slaughter weight; their meat is leaner.) And people (most people) have gotten used to the taste of corn-fed beef. And like it.

"Without cheap corn," Mr. Pollan says, "the modern urbanization of livestock would probably never have occurred." Perhaps his most damning statement is that "many of the health problems associated with eating beef are really problems with corn-fed beef." Oh no, maybe this is even worse: "The short unhappy life of a corn-fed feedlot steer represents the ultimate triumph of industrial thinking over the logic of evolution." And it's not just how the animals are raised—it's how they live and how they die. Which, if you can believe it, is even worse. Ironically, what keeps a feedlot animal healthy is antibiotics. Antibiotics are used to treat sick animals who, Mr. Pollan points out, probably wouldn't be sick in the first place if they hadn't been fed all that corn and crammed together in those feedlots.

And if you think the animals are unhealthy, there's this: meat from corn-fed beef contains more saturated fat and fewer omega-3 fatty acids than that of grass-fed animals. Grass-fed beef has a lower total fat content than grain-fed beef—so low it's closer to the levels in skinless chicken breasts. It's also higher in vitamin C and in vitamin E, which is linked to a lower risk of heart disease. As for

With surgical precision and a craftsman's eye, head butcher
T. J. Burnham trims the fat at Marlow & Daughters.

the environment, a sustainable farm Web site notes that feeding grain to animals contributes heavily to today's large-scale industrial methods of farming, including the devastation that agricultural petrochemicals wreak on the soil and on the water. Grass fed and grain finished is a compromise method that is frequently used these days. (Finishing, by the way, is a livestock term that refers to how animals are fattened 90 to 160 days before slaughter, whether on grass or grain.) Young animals graze in pastures for most of their lives and are given grain at the end of their lives. The goal of the rancher is to fatten them up a little more and make sure their meat has more marbling. Which will—bottom line—fatten their cost.

Marlow & Daughters, a butcher shop with a conscience in Brooklyn, New York, was kind enough to let me watch head butcher T. J. Burnham break down beef one day. And interview him mid-cut. All the beef sold at Marlow & Daughters is grass fed, and Burnham is no fan of corn fed. "By logic," he told me, "a corn-fed animal is on the verge of a natural death when it is led to slaughter. And its immune system is pretty much destroyed by all the antibiotics." I asked him how he felt about grass fed, grain finished, and he admitted that he had no problem with the taste: "It does give a sweetness to it." He also pointed out that the lack of strict laws and the absence of clear language about raising cattle can not only confuse but mislead: "Since there is no USDA definition for grass fed, technically, a farmer can finish his cattle for 90 to 160 days on grain. But he can call it 'grass fed' if it's finished on grain. Although most grass-fed cattle ranchers are ethical and humane, this is not always true and cannot be assumed based upon a grass-fed label. So just because it's called 'grass fed' doesn't mean that it's humanely raised."

Is grass fed the answer? Grass fed is, for many people, the gold standard for outstanding taste and upstanding practices. One of the chief proponents (can you say messianic?) is writer/environmentalist/ethicist/savant Michael Pollan who introduced us to the shocking and specific horrors of CAFOs: Concentrated Animal Feeding Operations. Alice Waters spoke for many when, in a 2010 *Time* magazine article about *The Omnivore's Dilemma*, she said, "It's a harrowing tale, and since the moment I heard him tell it, I have not served corn-fed beef of any kind. I was Pollanized—and I am not alone." Mr. Pollan himself told me that brisket "is a great grass-fed cut (since tenderness ceases to be an issue)."

And yet not everyone agrees. California's well-respected Brandt Beef Ranch (Brooklyn's Fatty 'Cue has used their meat) Web site says that "they are a premium natural beef producer" and "that every animal on the Brandt ranch is fed a corn-based vegetarian diet." Brandt's executive chef, Tom McAliney, boasts that with their meat, "you get a full flavor that I've never yet had from steaks that are just grass-fed," adding, "I have yet to see a strictly grass-fed beef rated choice or prime." Yet, talk to other ranchers and butchers and you will hear them say flat out that they disagree and believe that Brandt's grain-fed meat is neither premium nor natural. Talk to barbecue writer Ardie Davis, who has been all over the country researching his cookbooks and competing on the circuit, and he will tell you, "Thus far I haven't found a single barbecuer who has success with totally grass-fed beef." Josh Baum, chef/owner of Josh's Barbecue in Santa Fe, New Mexico, agrees. He told me, "My beef is New Mexico grown, grass fed, but finished with grain before processing."

But how does grass-fed beef taste? Well, it depends on your taste. Some people like what they perceive as a deeper, meatier flavor. Some believe all grass is too intense a taste, the meat is too lean, and it's not juicy enough. An online food critic says, "It tastes uneven, just as you might expect the meat of a nonindustrial animal to taste." "It tastes better than corn-fed beef: meatier, purer, far less fatty, the way we imagine beef tasted before feedlots and farm subsidies changed ranchers and cattle," says author and respected food writer Corby Kummer in an *Atlantic Monthly* piece called "Back to Grass." A Pennsylvania farm family's Web site gives a mixed review: "Our family is divided: some of us prefer the sweet, rich taste of grain fed while others prefer the leaner, more complex taste of grass fed." Whole Foods's Web site sums up their advocacy of grass-fed beef with this oddly jolly tribute: "Grass-fed beef is a delicious alternative to grain-fed beef and cooks a little differently. Wow those hungry mouths."

Fatty 'Cue pit master Robbie Richter says it isn't so simple—that a label can't begin to accurately predict the exact taste. "No matter what it is raised on—with the exception of a feedlot cow that's 100 percent corn fed—you gotta expect that there is going to be great variation in taste texture, size, and portion," he told me. "It's going to vary from animal to animal, seasons, local growing conditions, weather, what's plentiful in the field. This is quality beef. It's not Chicken McNuggets." Every butcher I spoke to cared deeply about not only finding a great source for beef but for sharing this with the person who was going to buy or eat it. Tom Mylan on Serious Eats says it all: "If you don't know where your meat comes from, then you probably don't want to know where your meat comes from."

Corn fed. Grass fed. Pasture fed. Vermont fed. Food writer Regina Schrambling is just fed up. And she's feeling bad. "There's no way to write about eating meat these days without offending someone," Schrambling says on Epicurious.

"I'll just plunge in and say we're guiltier than ever before. A farmer at our neighborhood Greenmarket recently seduced us with his grass-fed beef, and it's so good we seem to be buying once a week, either from him or from the supermarket, which now carries grass-fed meat as well. And we almost never bought beef before."

Oh, Regina. You don't need to do The Walk of Shame every time you think you should buy the chicken but wind up with a slab of beef in your eco-friendly recycled tote bag. I've decided this is an area where everyone just needs to agree to disagree. And respect someone else's choice. Or as zen master T. J. Burnham diplomatically puts it, "You're the only one who ultimately decides what you put into your mouth and your body."

"It varies from animal to animal; seasons; local growing conditions; weather; what's plentiful in the field. This is quality beef. It's not Chicken McNuggets."

—Robbie Richter, Pit Master, Fatty 'Cue

The whole brisket and nothing but the brisket: the pride of pitmaster Robbie Richter, who in turn is the pride of Brooklyn's Fatty 'Cue.

"If you don't know where your meat comes from, then you probably don't want to know where your meat comes from."

—Tom Mylan, butcher, seriouseats.com

Supermarket meat with its wealth of variety, and dearth of information.

From Birth to Death to Temple Grandin

Nicolette Hahn Niman argues that, when it comes to feeding practices, Michael Pollan has missed a crucial point. "The real issue," she says," has to do with when cattle go into feedlots—and there has been a major shift that occurred in the last century. The animals are much younger now when they are slaughtered. They used to be put in feedlots when they were around five years old. Now they can be as young as a year and a half. Since we've left Niman Ranch, we're raising fully mature cattle, all on grass, and getting a great response. Using older cattle makes it possible to do grass fed. They are fattened on grass and slaughtered seasonally."

It is worth addressing how animals are slaughtered. There are two issues: one is concern for treating animals humanely from birth to death. The other is the growing belief that the meat from a panicky, about-to-be-slaughtered animal will not be as tender as one who is killed in a more natural and less stressful way. The genius behind more enlightened slaughter practices is Temple Grandin. She is a passionate animal welfare activist, the leading American designer of commercial slaughterhouses, and has single-handedly changed an industry. Her autism gives her a gift: the ability to see the world from the cow's point of view. She believes that fear is one of the main emotions of a person with autism and also one of the main emotions of animals.

Meet the Meat. Meet the Butcher.

The Eight Primal Cuts. What would have previously sounded to me like a samurai movie started to make sense once I began frequenting new-style old-school butchers, reading nose-to-tail chefs like Fergus Henderson, and discovered that Francophile author Julie Powell had stopped reconstructing Julia Child and started deconstructing large animals in what seems to be the new glam-girl, macho career. Ms. Powell, in her book *Cleaving*, mentions wearing her work T-shirt with the company slogan, "You can't beat our meat." Too cool for school.

But back to our main feature, starring Brisket: The Eight Primal Cuts.

Chuck/Shoulder	Round	Rib
Brisket/Shank	Short Loin	Plate
Sirloin	Flank	

These are the cuts of beef sold at wholesale. And from this first series of primal cuts, a butcher will make the cuts you buy at retail. Brisket comes from the chest of the animal. (A whole brisket averages around ten pounds.) Butchers generally cut the brisket crosswise in half. So there are two briskets. The flatter, leaner one is called the "flat." The encyclopedic Virtual Weber Bullet site (virtualweberbullet.com), which is not related to the official Weber site, says that "from an anatomical perspective, the brisket flat is the 'deepest' portion of meat and is attached to the rib cage, while the brisket point sits on top of the flat and is nearest the surface." The point is thicker and fattier. The flat has some fat but is far leaner.

Then, there is the deckle, which is the fat and muscle that attach the brisket flat to the rib cage of the animal. The point is often called the deckle, especially in barbecue circles. A whole, untrimmed brisket—both flat and point—that comes in the Cryovac packaging is referred to as packer cut and is what is almost always used for barbecuing. A packer will have fat running through the middle and on top to keep the brisket moist while cooking.

There are a variety of other names and terms. Some are regional, some are butcher terms, and some are just there to make it more confusing to figure out what to look for or ask for.

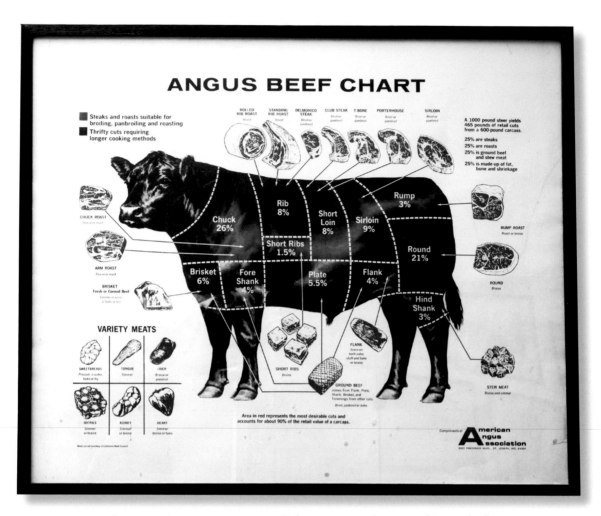

Brisket, states this vintage poster, is a thrifty cut requiring longer cooking methods.

FYI: The flat of the brisket is also called the "first cut," "thin cut," "nose off," or "cap removed." The point is also known as the "second cut," "thick cut," "nose cut," "front cut," or "cap left on." The packer cut is also called packer trimmed. In Australia, Ireland, and New Zealand, "silverside" is the name of the cut of choice for making corned beef.

Braising a brisket brings out the most ardent proponents and opponents of a particular cut, and a lot of this has to do with how much fat should be on the brisket, both pre- and post-cooking. Brisket barbecuers and the corned beef people have managed to pretty much agree on what works best. Or they just ask their wives. From a forum on barbecuenews.com: "Personally, I don't find cooking 'flat only' to be less work. Just less time. In my experience, the results are never as good. And most important, my wife, who loves the point, would kill me."

The reason you need to separate the flat from the point if you have cooked them as a whole is that brisket has to be sliced across the grain. When the point and flat are attached, the grain runs in different directions. In our butchering session at Marlow & Daughters, T. J. Burnham told me, "It's the graining and the fat structure that makes brisket brisket. Not unlike skirt or flank, brisket has a real graining structure." His interesting observation—one you might want to use for your next Brisket Trivia Night: "Everything except beef jerky is cut against the grain. Beef jerky is cut with the grain to maximize its toughness."

What makes brisket such a tough cut? The rule is that the closer a cut is to the back of the animal, the more tender it will be. The meat in the forequarters—like brisket, chuck, and round—is tougher because meat is muscle. And the animal uses the muscles in the front of the body more often and more vigorously than it uses those in the back. Front muscles get the most exercise; walking, grazing, lying down, standing up. Once you understand that these muscles are tougher, it makes sense that they benefit from long, slow, moist heat cooking methods that will loosen their connective tissue.

To be a bit more technical, thanks to chem whiz Molly Stevens, from her book, *All About Braising*: "All muscles contain some amount of collagen, often referred to as connective tissue, because collagen is what binds muscles to one another." She points out that tough cuts like brisket contain a lot of collagen. "Anything else in the process?" I asked Kenji Lopez-Alt. He says that "as you cook, proteins come out and flavor the water. Collagen breaks down and forms gelatin. In other words, muscle fibers tighten up and moisture comes out." That, he adds, explains the need for a low cooking temperature and the "low and slow" mantra.

BRISKET FOR ROOKIES

Me & T. J.

The most helpful local visits I made in my brisket year were a number of field trips to Fatty 'Cue to eat everything in sight . . . I mean, to interview Chef Zak Pelaccio and pit master Robbie Richter . . . as well as my afternoon of butchering with T. J. Burnham at Marlow & Daughters Traditional Butcher. Happily, these two shrines to brisket are within walking distance. You can burn off at least twelve brisket calories going from one to the other.

At Marlow & Daughters I got to see a cheerful and spotless butcher shop that is just the opposite of any kind of dark Dickensian place I might have imagined. No bloody butcher aprons, no whining sound of falling limbs, no greasy floor strewn with reject scraps. No one singing Sweeney Todd, "Hold your razor high, Sweeney!" If this place hasn't been in *Martha Stewart Living* yet, it's only a question of time. Sunny, spotless, cheerful. Chic. On one side, a meat case filled with local pastured meat—offerings so fresh, artisanal, and inviting that a vegan would find it hard to resist the robust sausages or the rabbit pâté. And then there was well-marbled T. J. (fine, he does look like he could be on *People* magazine's annual list of sexiest men) and his crew—having done some pre-butchering to cut down the brisket so we could see what it looked like, where it came from on the animal, and the fat that's on it. "The fat translates to moisture," T. J. said. I asked him how he got started. "I came from a culinary background. I was at a steak house and moved on. I gravitated to meat cutting." He describes his way of breaking down as a Zen way of butchering. "I ask the animal how it would like to be broken down." T. J.'s POV on barbecued brisket is kind of Zen, too. "If you baste it too much it dries out. If you baste it too little, it dries out."

Naturally, I was curious about how he would advise making choices about buying beef. "I'd go for local grass fed before I'd go for certified organic—partly that has to do with the carbon footprint." And then, as I watched, he explained what he was doing:

1. Take off the external skin
2. Expose the brisket
3. Sever a tendon
4. Easily pull off the brisket

"I ask the animal how it would like to be broken down."

—T.J. Burnham, head butcher, Marlow & Daughters

He added that the more you cut, the more the natural seam shows. So we saw the seams in a whole huge brisket. Then we separated it into the flat and the point. Lest it seem confusing, the flat does happen to be flat. And the point really does come to a point. One of the best things I learned was noticing the singular streaks of fat right in the middle of the whole animal: "What's that?" I asked T. J. "That's what we call 'wiggle meat,' the external muscle that cows build up when they are moving to repel flies" was the reply. Who wouldn't love a highly skilled butcher who demonstrates the anatomy of a cut of meat, explains what "wiggle meat" is, and shrugs off your compliments by joking, "Isn't a surgeon just a butcher who's good at exams?"

Me & Zak & Robbie

What can I say? No matter what you are eating at Fatty 'Cue, you find yourself saying, "Oh my God, this is the best [NAME OF FOOD HERE] I ever had." It's also the best food you never knew existed: "Dragon Pullman Toast/side of master fat?" Fatty 'Cue is possibly the trendiest restaurant in Brooklyn (is that redundant?) There's nothing particularly great looking about it—except for the hulking smokers outside the kitchen door and the sublime juiciness of what's on your plate. Or dribbling down your shirt. This place is so beyond hip that it wows by both its understated intentions and by the absolute knockout punch of its crazy amazing food combos. South Carolina marries Pankor Laut: "Heritage Pork Ribs: Smoked fish-palm syrup, Indonesian red pepper."

On its Web site: "Fatty 'Cue is an effort by a few of the members of the Fatty Crew to bring to Brooklyn a little Southeast Asian fermented funkiness and a whole helluva lot of smoke." If their goal is "to balance quivering fatty morsels of deliciousness with bright citrus notes, fiery chili heat, rich fermented and briny washes and complex, unrefined, natural sweetness," they succeed. No, they exceed. This is not the place to go if you are against superlatives, adjectives, or ikan bilis. Raves *The New Yorker*: "Best of all, sheets of thinly sliced brisket, to be stuffed into chubby bao, or buns, then dipped in house-made aioli and smothered in sweet chile jam."

I have a short talk with Chef Zak Pelaccio while I'm eating. I ask him for any insight into brisket. He says, "My girlfriend's from Austin. Her father cooks a great brisket. What makes it great? First, the meat. Then the smoker." Why, I ask, isn't there more barbecue in New York? Zak tells me that "the problem with beef today is that if you're not doing nose to tail, there's no space." Speaking of space: a *New York Times* article pointed out that Fatty 'Cue's "side yard, where cords of oak are stacked, is shared by a small structure that houses Veronica Schwartz's tiny vegan kitchen where she produces nut milk cheeses for restaurants and shops. 'It's funny, but what can I do,' she says of being next to a temple of meat."

While I'm not wolfing something down with Zak, I ask pit boss Robbie Richter some questions out by the smoker. Robbie presides over two Ole Hickory smokers, which can smoke approximately 400 pounds of meat at a time. By the time we've finished I smell like smoke. Eau de Fatty 'Cue. Yum. One of the best things about Robbie, aside from his passion and skill, is that he started barbecuing on weekends in his backyard in Queens, New York. Now—though he's only a few miles from where he's started—he's world famous. He started his own team, competed in over fifty barbecue competitions, and won over 150 awards.

Fatty 'Cue's award-winning brisket sandwich. See the recipe for the sandwich's sauce—revealed for the first time!—on p.146.

ME: "Where does a home barbecuer start? It's kind of daunting. Especially brisket."

ROBBIE: "It used to be—when I first started—that Home Depot would have one grill. Now there's half a dozen smokers. And the Internet is great. I'll throw a shout-out to The BBQ Forum and to The Virtual Weber Bullet. They're really helpful sites. You can learn a lot. Also, you can get pretty professional results with the Weber Bullet (that's the lower end) and The Big Green Egg (higher end). I've used both at home."

ME: "What not to do?"

ROBBIE: "No Liquid Smoke. If you're barbecuing properly you don't need it. Get wood chips instead."

ME: "How to succeed?"

ROBBIE: "Look up and follow The Minion Method. It's named after Jim Minion and it is the best way to achieve a low and slow temperature, letting your coals burn down slowly. And use natural briquettes. I like Kingsford and Wicked Good."

ME: "Sauces?"

ROBBIE: "Look up sauces on hawgeyesbbq.com. I like Blues Hog. Use Smokin' Guns on your brisket and you're almost guaranteed to place (smokingunsbbq.com)."

ME: "What kind of brisket do you smoke?"

ROBBIE: "We use the packer—the whole brisket—then take it apart once it's done. Just using the flat is a little problematic—it can get too dry and ropey. And then it does depend on where you are getting your beef from—ours is from Brandt—the only family ranch in California. You can buy from Costco or Fresh Direct—but no feedlot beef."

ME: "Should you buy kosher brisket?"

ROBBIE: "Because it's already soaked and salted, it starts to brine. And that might be fine for brined brisket but it isn't for barbecue."

ME: "Advice to novice barbecuers?"

ROBBIE: "Brisket is a commitment in time. Be patient. Keep a low temperature and don't trim the fat."

ME: "Where should non–pit masters buy their brisket?"

ROBBIE: "It's easy to order brisket online from sustainable resources. My theory about justifying spending that money is that we all eat too much meat. So when you do, go ahead and buy meat that is sustainable. I haven't bought a piece of meat in a supermarket in a decade."

ME: "If you don't barbecue it, what else can you do with brisket?"

ROBBIE: "What else can you do with the cut? You can make corned beef or pastrami. But let me tell you, there are corned beefs and pastramis that should have stayed briskets."

LEAVE IT ALONE! IT'S GONNA DRY OUT! OH, STOP, IT'S FINE. LET IT COOK! 350? NO! 325? I SHOULD I CHECK IT AGAIN?

4 Basic Training

"Boy. I dunno.
Came out like dried shoe leather."

—*food52.com post*

While brisket is plentiful, confidence is not. I first noticed this when I was researching this book and started to talk about nothing but brisket with my friends. They'd ask, "How was your weekend?" And I would say something like, "We saw the Sophia Coppola movie. Did you know that Gil Marks—the historian who wrote the book on Jewish cooking—said that more Jews eat sushi and salsa today than schmaltz?" If they feigned interest I would add that J. Kenji Lopez-Alt told me that he wouldn't be surprised if more people used Lipton Onion Soup Mix in their briskets than real onions. (How hard core am I getting? Just about every day, I get an online industry newsletter called meatingplace so I can keep up. Today's big headlines were: "Second month of record U.S. meat production" and "Russia bans German pigs . . .").

What came out of this was a) my friends' concern that perhaps I was getting a little obsessive about brisket and b) their not entirely mistaken belief that I have turned into someone who really knows a lot about this subject. I'm now thought of as a person to freely share brisket anxieties with. "Why is MY brisket tough?" they ask me with the same anguish they'd use for a question about their marriage. "How can I make it really tender?" "Do you think he'll think less of me if I tell him I make mine with Campbell's Soup?" "If my mother ruined her brisket, does that mean I will?" And the almost universal one: "Can you give me a recipe from your book? An EASY one?"

Honestly, I feel their pain and share their concern. You can ruin a steak, but that only takes ten minutes or so. When you screw up a brisket, you will have probably put in at least four hours total for a braised brisket and maybe fifteen hours for a barbecued one. Or waited two weeks or

"Brisket is one nasty cut of meat. It will fight you ferociously as you try to tame it. Once you do, though, it lays down like a cuddly puppy and rewards you with a big, delicious hug."

—Danny Meyer, restaurateur

so to see how your corned beef turned out. Not to mention the angst of buying the meat, betting on a good recipe, getting up early to defrost or staying up late to baste, and most daunting of all, expecting lots of your loved ones to come over and eat it.

It's not just my friends who need brisket advice and support—go online and you will see pleas for help only matched by the poignancy of plover rescue groups. "Help! Brisket gravy almost gone!" from Epicurious. "When I made the brisket, the plastic melted!" from Ina Garten's Web site. "Smoked whole brisket—covered in mold?" on Chowhound.

And let me tell you, if Danny Meyer—America's restaurant emperor and owner of Blue Smoke, New York's shining beacon of barbecue—agrees that there's reason to be concerned, you know it's not just you having a neurotic brisket day. Danny told me how much he loves brisket: "Brisket is one nasty cut of meat. It will fight you ferociously as you try to tame it. Once you do, though, it lays down like a cuddly puppy and rewards you with a big, delicious hug."

But how to tame it? I went to the best cooks, cookbooks, food chemists, restaurateurs, and competitive barbecuers hoping they would have all the answers. They do have answers, but not alas, always the same answers. With brisket, sometimes you have to make your own call. I asked these wizards if they could throw a little encouragement in with their advice. Which they did, for no extra charge. (It helps to remember that it was only a dozen or so years ago that Washington, D.C., chef Todd Gray made his first braised brisket. And look how well he's done. Of course, maybe it didn't hurt that Todd is a genius cook to begin with.)

Here is my distillation of brisket basics from people who really know. People who want you to succeed. Brisket, braised, barbecued, brined, served FAQ style:

Q. **Browning.** *Cook's Illustrated* recommends browning the meat before you braise it. Joan Nathan says brown it only if you have time. Barbara Kafka roasts hers before slow cooking it on top of the stove. Pioneer Woman (Ree Drummond) doesn't brown her Passover brisket. Nor does *The Joy of Cooking*'s Brisket with Sauerkraut. Who's right?

A. Maybe everybody. "Chemistry is complex," says Kenji Lopez-Alt. "Browning is still a complete mystery. We have never mapped out the actual process."

Q. **So should you? Do you?**

A. Kenji: "If you brown before you braise or barbecue, you increase the flavor. But you desiccate the outer layer of the meat. So—the browned one will be juicier than the non-browned, but slightly drier on the exterior. It's a trade-off a cook has to make: browned and more flavor vs. a slightly drier exterior."

Q. **So Kenji, how come so many braised brisket recipes include onions?**

A. "There is a simple alchemy between onions and meat since both proteins and sugar are essential to developing the complex flavors of cooked brisket. Onions and brisket are a perfect combination."

French chemist Louis-Camille Maillard

(If you want to check out a felicitous chemical attraction, Google "the Maillard reaction," which is also known as "the browning reaction." And an aside: the Web site The Accidental Scientist (exploratorium.edu) notes that scientists studying the Maillard reaction discovered that as many as six hundred components have been identified in the aroma of beef.)

Q. **What actually happens when brisket cooks—how does this tough cut turn tender?**

A. Kenji: "As you cook, two important things happen. Collagen slowly breaks down and forms gelatin, while muscle fibers tighten up and squeeze out moisture into your cooking liquid,

Homemade corned beef from Liehs & Steigerwald in Syracuse, New York. This pampered brisket is cured for no less than two weeks with water, salt, sodium nitrate, and a blend of seasonings.

flavoring it. You need to cook it low and slow. Low, because high temperatures will cause the muscle fibers to squeeze too hard, drying out the meat, and slow, because collagen takes plenty of time to break down properly."

Q. **So it goes right from tough to tender?**

A. "No. It starts out tender, then toughens as it approaches the 160 to 180°F zone. As collagen breaks down, it becomes tender again. You can eat it at the early tender stages in Korean restaurants where it's sliced thinly and sizzled briefly over hot coals." Who knew? Kenji knows.

Q. **Why is this cut so tough that you have to wrestle it into submission?**

A. "The problem with beef brisket," says food scientist Guy Crosby, "is that it contains more connective tissue and collagen than any other primal cut of meat, and is second only to the level of collagen in the skin." No wonder we like brisket. We're *like* brisket!

What to look for when you prepare brisket for braising?

A.   No one puts it more poetically than British chef Fergus Henderson in his book *The Whole Beast: Nose to Tail Eating:* "You are looking for an iceberg effect: part of the beef is not covered but we know there is a lot more submerged in the stock."

Q.   **Corned beef gets its pink color from nitrates. Good? Not so good? Toxic?**

A.   Kenji reassures: "Nitrates fix the pigment (myloglobin). It's a natural pigment." The editors of *Cook's Illustrated* tested lots of commercial corned beef for *The New Best Recipe* to come up with their favorite. Their conclusion? Gray corned beef has superior flavor and they note, "for that, we'll gladly trade the color pink."

From an e-mail to Boston food scientist Guy Crosby. He expands on what Kenji has to say about the tenderizing process:

Q.   **Me to Guy: "It seems to me that the overriding problem for both a home cook and a home barbecuer is getting brisket that is dry, tough, ropey. And the main reasons for dry brisket (this goes for braising and barbecue) would be not cooking it at a low enough temperature or not cooking it long enough. Two additional reasons for a disappointing braised brisket would be not having enough liquid to keep it moist and not using an ingredient sweet enough (onions, ketchup, brown sugar, etc.) to successfully work the protein + sugar combination that is essential. Would you say this is true?"**

Haiku for Braising Brisket

Low

Slow

Onions

Haiku for Barbecuing Brisket

Low

Slow

Maybe a Rub

A.   Guy to Me: "What you say is true. Any way of adding or retaining moisture during the long slow cooking process will help. In meat, all the muscle fibers are encased in connective tissue, which is mostly made of the protein collagen. As the meat heats the connective tissue shrinks and squeezes the bundles of encased muscle fibers, forcing moisture out of the fibers. The key is to heat the meat just high enough to begin to break down the collagen to gelatin (above 160°F) but not so high (less than 200°F) that the connective tissue shrinks so much that excessive moisture is squeezed out of the muscle fibers. Further, what moisture is squeezed out of the fibers needs to be retained by the gelatin rather than evaporated."

He goes on to say that "low and slow" is crucial and then adds this brief, brilliant tactical directive: "Too much heat is the enemy." Keep calm and carry on!

BARBECUED BRISKET: The Basics

"If pork is Barbecuing 101, brisket is like a senior seminar with a cranky-ass professor" reads a been-there, done-that barbecue post on Chowhound.

An observation: The barbecue people write a lot more colorfully than the braised brisket people. The corned beef people hardly write at all, except when St. Patrick's Day is approaching. This is not an atypical piece of online advice from someone who refers to himself as a 2010 world-class Texas barbecue brisket champ: "Remember to establish good steady heat inside the cooker. A cold brisket is a lot like a stubborn jackass; sometimes you have to hit el burro in the head with a two-by-four to get his attention." Dang!

And as mentioned before, aside from some really excellent barbecue books, some of the very best advice you'll get is online. A couple of terrific and comprehensive sites: virtualweberbullet.com (which is not the official Weber site), barbecueforum.com, and cookshack.com.

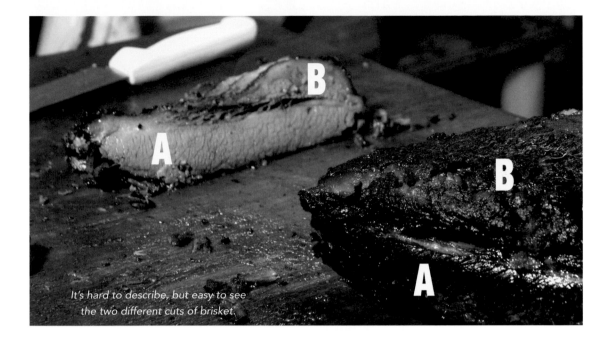

It's hard to describe, but easy to see the two different cuts of brisket.

The Flat and The Point

From AmazingRibs.com, the world's most popular barbecue Web site.

I love this site. It's run by by the equally amazing "Meathead," who has one name and a million helpful recipes, insights, ideas, and tips.

I asked him, what's the point?

His answer: "You can see the two muscles in this whole packer brisket at the legendary Black's Barbecue in Lockhart, Texas, where they've been smoking brisket since 1932. The flat is labeled 'A' in the photo and the point is labled 'B.'"

The horizontal line along the side of the piece at right is the fat layer that separates the point from the flat. You can also see the fat line in the tip that has been cut off at left. Notice that this tip is mostly flat, with only a thin layer of point. Notice, also, the dark mahogany black crust, the amber fat cap below the cracking crust on the point at right, and the pink smoke ring below the crust on the piece on the left."

BARBECUE Q&A

Q. **Do you use the flat or the point or the whole brisket?**

A. Texas barbecue expert Robb Walsh told me, "Many Northerners attempt to barbecue the kind of trimmed brisket you find in the grocery store up there. It doesn't work. For barbecue you must use a packer's cut brisket—one that still has all of the natural fat attached. The fat cap on a brisket is roughly equal in weight to the meat, so if the brisket to be barbecued doesn't weigh ten pounds or so, something is wrong."

Brian Perrone stands in front of Slows in the Corktown neighborhood of Detroit. First, Slows revitalized barbecue, then it helped revitalize Detroit. Way to go, Slows!

Chef Brian Perrone from Slows in Detroit agrees. "I cook whole briskets with a pretty thick fat cap and both muscles connected, the point and the flat. There is so much intramuscular fat in the point that it helps protect the flat when cooking." Ditto Richard Westhaver, from Norwell, Massachusetts. He's a competitive barbecuer who heads the team Dirty Dick and the Legless Wonders. Richard has been on the circuit for almost thirty years. (Google his amazing hot sauce, Dickie's Sweet Bird.) Richard says, "No one in the barbecue world is cooking a flat. If I can, I get an eighteen-pound brisket. From thirty years of looking for meat like that, I know you have to go to a restaurant supply place or maybe BJ's or special-order from a butcher." (If he says pretty much the same thing as Fatty 'Cue pit master Robbie Richter, that's probably because he was one of Robbie's mentors.)

Q. **Wait, what's the "fat cap" again?**

A. From Robb Walsh: "The layer of fat on top of a packer's cut is called the fat cap. It should be about an inch thick to keep the brisket moist while it is cooking."

(Quick review: A packer's cut is the entire brisket: the point and the flat together. So the fat cap sits on top of the point, which sits on top of the flat. They are connected through a thinner layer of connective fat. Barbecuers do not separate these two pieces.)

Q. **Is a "smoker" the same thing as a "grill"? If it's not, do you need both? Or can you turn your grill into a smoker and vice versa? If so, how?**

A. Ardie Davis says, "For the barbecue books we ("we" being Ardie and chef Paul Kirk—aka The Baron of Barbecue and seven-time world barbecue champion) wrote for one publisher (Harvard Common Press), we called it a grill for the sake of consistency."

Q. **So, you don't need a separate smoker?**

A. "No, but modifications are needed," he says, "to smoke in a standard grill. Put the coals on one side of the grill and the brisket opposite."

Q. **What about barbecue sauce on brisket?**

A. Ardie Davis says, "I want to hear guests say, 'This brisket is so good it needs no sauce.' Since there are so many good sauces already out there, I seldom make sauce from scratch. A few favorites I will serve on the side are Arthur Bryant's Original, KC Baron of BBQ Original, and Cowtown."

Many teams have their own rubs, mops, and sauces and sell them online. The Steven Raichlen book *Barbecue! Bible: Sauces, Rubs, and Marinades, Bastes, Butters, and Glazes* from Workman is a great source. So is *Paul Kirk's Championship Barbecue* with a subtitle that's as loquacious as Paul isn't: *"Barbecue Your Way to Greatness with 575 Lip-Smackin' Recipes from the Baron of Barbecue."*

Fatty 'Cue's pit master Robbie Richter says, "Sure, there are good ones. Lots of competitive barbecuers have their own. Blues Hog is one.

Love Letters to The Big Green Egg

Just about everyone I interviewed agreed with Richard Westhaver's recommendations: the 22-inch Weber Smokey Mountain Grill and the Big Green Egg, which he uses at home. And Richard offered some good news, especially for insomniacs.

Richard: "You can cook a killer brisket at home."

Me: "How?"

Richard: "You have to stay up all night. I put my brisket on the smoker at 10:00 P.M. Then I get up every three hours. It's like having a baby in the house."

Me: "And you don't have to send it to college."

If that's not win-win, I don't know what is. The Big Green Egg is a ceramic smoker based on an ancient Asian-style clay cooker called a kamado. It is indeed big, green, and egg-shaped. It looks to me like Dr. Seuss had a role in its design. If you want to see five-star rave reviews, go to Amazon or Sam's Club. Or speak to an Egghead at an Eggfest.

One of the reasons the Big Green Egg is so loved is its versatility. It can be used as a grill, a smoker, or an oven. It looks über-cool and Wikipedia makes it better by noting that it is "manufactured from high fiber ceramics developed for the space shuttle program."

So the astronomical price ($700 to $800) doesn't seem to faze its devoted fans.

Matthew Morgan is the co-owner of specialty food and wine store Morgan & York in Ann Arbor, Michigan. They smoke juicy briskets at least two or three times a week for parties, private clients, and hungry fans after a University of Michigan football game. Go, Blue! Matthew says, "I love the Egg. It does a great job, and the range of operating temperatures is terrific . . . Smoking with the Egg is so easy, it's hard to even think of any 'tips.' Use plenty of fuel, I guess—that way you don't have to refuel midday, and use aluminum foil or disposable pans to catch the drippings for easier cleanup."

Speaking of fans . . . from a Chowhound barbecue forum: "The Big Green Egg is perfect in every way. Marriages come and go. Mortgages implode. Car companies vanish overnight. Yet there, on the deck, sits the perfect cooking tool. Hurricane winds cannot move it; it works as a tornado shelter for small children. It makes any user into the next Bobby Flay . . ."

Love Letters to Weber

The black porcelain-coated Weber Smokey Mountain Cooker (think Johnny Cash) is a bullet-shaped charcoal water smoker. Unlike the Big Green Egg, it is only a smoker. Just about every barbecue site I went through says that while there are others to choose from, the Weber is the best. Straightforward, compact, no bells and whistles, it can smoke for up to twelve hours straight on one filling of charcoal briquets. It's also reasonable—a smaller model costs in the neighborhood of $300.

Not to be outdone by vocal Eggheads, the Weber has a splashy presence on Facebook and more pictures of smoking brisket in the snow than you can possibly imagine. Another Weber fan is *Cook's Illustrated*, whose 2010 review reads: "Save for its lack of handles, [the Weber Smokey Mountain Cooker] literally smoked the competition: plenty of cooking space, a water pan, and multiple vents that allowed for precise temperature control added up to meat that came off the fire consistently moist and smoky with little tending necessary."

An Amazon review: "This smoker is becoming the standard of the industry for bullet-type smokers. Many competition barbecue teams are winning contests using this simple unit. The cooker has the ability to run for over twelve hours on a single loading of briquets. Makes long cooks of brisket or butts quite easy."

Another excerpt from Amazon for the Weber Smokey Mountain: "Good quality and very easy to use. I fill up the charcoal and water and usually go fishing for the day . . . "

BARBECUE TOOLS

I asked Ardie Davis (who will also tell you the best barbecue places in Kansas City if you happen to run into him there) to share his toolkit. Here's his list of essentials:

- Leather welding gloves. Wear them to help prevent burns when grilling.

- A chimney starter. A convenient, safe way to light your coals and inexpensive to boot.

- A candy thermometer. If your grill doesn't have a temperature gauge, use this to monitor the interior heat level. Ardie, who has seen his share of what I can only call "pitfalls," suggests adhering the thermometer to the grill after you insert the bulb end into the top vent to ensure that it doesn't fall in.

- An instant-read meat thermometer. No bigger than a pencil, this ultra-portable gadget takes the guesswork out of when the brisket is done.

- A sturdy meat fork, large cutting board with a well, and a long, sharp knife.

He concludes, "To smoke a perfect brisket, you need time and patience." Note: It would also help to have Ardie's home phone number handy.

WHERE THERE'S LIQUID SMOKE, THERE'S FIRE.

If you want to hear barbecue people go crazy (I actually don't), just ask them about wrapping their meat in foil or mention Liquid Smoke. What is it about Liquid Smoke that makes brisket lovers apoplectic? The world is divided into two camps: the emphatic "yes." And "Are you kidding me? No!" Let's just say there is nothing low and slow about these dialogues/diatribes.

BBR (Before Brisket Research), I had no idea what Liquid Smoke was. It just sounded kind of chemical and vaguely unhealthy. (Of course, who am I to talk? I use Lipton Onion Soup Mix in my brisket.) I first discovered the raging controversy when I went on the Chowhound boards. Is Liquid Smoke the work of the devil? What comes out of it? And what, exactly, goes into it?

"Liquid Smoke is the most immediately recognizable bad flavor known to man . . . redolent . . . of creosote, formaldehyde, termite mounds, the tears of mendacious orphans, crawl spaces, the acidic musk of old age homes . . . and bad barbecue . . . "

—Josh Ozersky, seriouseats.com

What I discovered is that there are different kinds of Liquid Smoke. Some are natural products and some are made with lots of additives and flavorings. Kenji Lopez-Alt reassured me: "People make such a big deal out of it. They think it's artificial and it's not. The best brands (the bad ones add ingredients) just have water and a natural smoke flavor they get from particles of smoking meat on wood chips." NYU chemistry professor Kent Kirshenbaum, in an interview on slashfood .com, says he, too, thought it must be some horrible chemical concoction. But after examining it, Professor Kirshenbaum says, "Liquid Smoke is very simply smoke in water. Smoke usually comes as a vapor, but there are ways to condense it and turn it into liquid and that liquid can then be carried in water." He adds that Liquid Smoke is actually "safer (for human ingestion) than untreated wood smoke." Barbecue author Steven Raichlen sums it up: "It's made by dissolving real wood smoke in water."

BBQers Who Hate Liquid Smoke

"I say leave out the Liquid Smoke, what is that shit anyway?" A Chowhound blogger.

"Liquid Smoke just sort of gives me the willies." Another Chowhounder.

"Is there any brand of Liquid Smoke that doesn't taste like ass?" A Metafilter.com post.

"All I can tell you is that Liquid Smoke is the most immediately recognizable bad flavor known to man. It's redolent simultaneously of creosote, formaldehyde, termite mounds, the tears of mendacious orphans, crawl spaces, the acidic musk of old age homes, guano caves, vinegar, and bad barbecue. It's also an extremely common ingredient in barbecue sauces, which is one reason I hate them so much." But tell us what you really think . . . Josh Ozersky on Serious Eats.

BBQers Who Know What It Is But Don't Use It

ME: Liquid Smoke or no?

FATTY 'CUE PIT MASTER ROBBIE RICHTER: "No Liquid Smoke. If you're barbecuing properly, you don't need it. Get wood chips instead. One of the big mistakes of barbecuers is that they lay too much smoke on their food. And a meat like brisket just soaks it up."

THE GREAT FOIL DEBATES

Foil or no Foil. If you think the Liquid Smoke discussions are heated, get ready for the Great Foil Debates. Foil, by the way, is known to barbecuers who live outside of Texas as "The Texas Crutch." I'm not about to ask Texan Robb Walsh what they call it in Texas.

An online purist says, "We draw the line at cooking with foil. In Texas, they cook brisket in twenty layers of plastic wrap and put it in the oven. Just don't call it barbecue."

The Texas Crutch

Chef Brian Perrone of Slows in Detroit, who has spent years at the smoker, says: "I disagree with starting in foil. I think finishing in foil can work if the meat isn't overcooked. I don't think connective tissue is a big deal if the brisket is cooked slowly enough. Slow and low is the answer."

Kenji Lopez-Alt, as much a foodie as a food chemist, says: "I use it when I'm braising for a tighter seal but I don't use it for barbecue. Frankly, even with a tight lid you're going to lose some juice. But if you want to go all out, seal the brisket you're braising with foil."

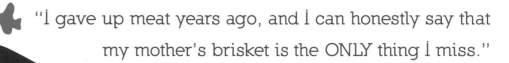

"I gave up meat years ago, and I can honestly say that my mother's brisket is the ONLY thing I miss."

—*Chowhound post*

BRAISING: What to Cook It In

A blogger on One for the Table, Amy Ephron's savvy and sunny food site, says, "Not many beef dishes guarantee such juiciness, unless you screw it up, which is pretty hard to do, unless you left the house and went to Antarctica and forgot about it."

Well, maybe there's a little more you need to know. For the basics—expertise about techniques, recipes, and tools—I turned primarily to the estimable Kathy Brennan (see Introduction) who braised all her briskets in her much-loved round red Le Creuset French oven, a pot that she says can practically last for generations.

Kenzi Lopez-Alt, in addition to being a managing editor, an author, an MIT graduate, and a food expert, also runs a private catering company. His preference, like Kathy Brennan's (well, like just about everybody's), is Le Creuset. Kenji also mentions less expensive options: Tramontina and Lodge. Lodge, by the way, is sold at Crate & Barrel and is almost $200 less than Le Creuset. The Tramontina is also much less pricey.

Read this tribute from the Walmart Web site for the Tramontina Dutch oven: "I had seen Tramontina reviewed by *Cook's Illustrated* in a comparison of cast-iron pots. They rated this a Best Buy because of the way it cooked and the price, compared to Le Creuset's price. It compared in everyway [sic]. We just cooked a pot roast in it, and had so much room for a lot more vegetables than usual. Glad we bought it."

So spend more on your brisket and less on your pot. Although there is something so iconic about Le Creuset, and no matter what color they make this lovely pot in, it seems like brisket and bright red go together.

BRAISING: What to Cook It *With*

Kathy Brennan's Toolbox

In her own words . . . and after slaving over a hot brisket for six months:

"When it comes to cooking moist, tender, flavorful brisket, the most important things you need—aside from an excellent piece of meat—are time and patience. They trump an arsenal of top-notch tools anytime. That said, there are a few pieces of equipment that will make the process easier. If you already have your own tried-and-true favorites, by all means continue to use them. As with brisket recipe preferences, the list below is subjective."

- An ovenproof enameled cast-iron pot with a tight-fitting lid. Whatever pot you use, make sure it is heavy and that the meat fits snugly. When braising, the liquid should cover about half to two-thirds of the meat; too much or two little space around the meat will affect how high the liquid comes up.

- An oven thermometer. Use this handy, inexpensive gadget to make sure your oven temperature is on the mark.

- A sturdy meat fork. Tongs are good for grabbing certain cuts of meat, but a meat fork is better suited for heavy, unwieldy pieces of brisket. Don't be concerned about piercing the meat and letting the juices out; according to Kenji Lopez, "Sometimes the brisket is so big it's easier to turn with a fork than tongs." When asked if it's bad to pierce it before/while it's cooking through, Kenji said, "A brisket is not a water balloon. Juice loss will be minimal if you stick a fork in. That's because brisket is a series of tubes filled with juice. Your fork might burst one or two but not all."

- A large cutting board with a well. You want plenty of room when slicing brisket and a built-in groove to catch the juices.

- A long, sharp knife. Briskets are usually large and have a tendency to shred when you slice them, particularly around the edges, so a short, dull knife won't get you very far. A ten-inch Henckels Granton Edge Slicer, which has small hollow-ground indentations along the blade to reduce friction, is ideal, but a good carving knife is fine. If you have an electric carving knife hiding in a drawer, now is the time to break it out; this is the perfect job for it.

Kathy's Recipe Tips

- If a recipe doesn't specify first- or second-cut brisket, use the type you prefer. First cut refers to the brisket flat. Second cut refers to the brisket point. Some like one better than the other. And people tend to make the assumption that "first" is superior to "second." The first cut is leaner and the second fattier and more marbleized. Prepare to be confused, however. Even top butchers are. "I prefer," said one of the expert butchers we worked with, "the point end of the flat."

- Both the brisket flat and the brisket point should be available with some fat on them. When a "trimmed" brisket is called for, trim the fat to about ¼ inch. You do not want to cook a brisket with no fat whatsoever on it. Then, it is a question of taste: some people prefer to serve their finished brisket with a little fat still on it; others trim it off before slicing it.

- The meat can be sliced thick or thin; it's up to you. Just be sure to slice it against (perpendicular to) the grain so it's not tough and stringy. Always slice your brisket against the grain is as much a mantra as "low and slow."

- Like a soup or stew, brisket generally tastes better a day or so after it's made.

  If possible, keep it in the refrigerator in the pot you cooked it in, with the lid tight. The meat should stay in the gravy or juices it was cooked in. Alternatively, you can store the cooked brisket in the refrigerator in the pot or pan you will use to reheat it.

- If the sauce is not as thick or full-flavored as you like, reduce it in a pan over medium heat.

CORNED BEEF

Liehs & Steigerwald have been corning their own briskets since 1936. They like, they say, to do things the old-fashioned way.

If braising brisket is relatively doable and barbecuing it is relatively daunting, where does that leave making your own corned beef? I asked expert cook Colman Andrews—who did years of research on Irish cooking for his book, *The Country Cooking of Ireland*—whether you should buy a corned beef or make your own. "I would say, 'Don't do it.' The reason I wouldn't is that I know the butcher will do it better. Let the experts make it. Of course," Colman added, "the problem is that corned beef is always more available around St. Patrick's Day. But your butcher can probably get it." Galumphs a Chowhound blogger who had just finished making Julia Child's corned beef brisket: "It's a commitment."

Cook's Illustrated, never one to shirk the task, did corn their own. And they note that their research "turned up two methods of corning—the wet cure and the dry cure. Both methods," they say, "require close to a week, but they are also mindlessly easy." Ingredients in this mindlessly easy but remarkably unsexy recipe include a two-gallon bag and two bricks.

A blogger who makes homemade corned beef has a sensible suggestion: "Make an extra one and coat it in cracked black pepper and coriander seeds, then smoke and steam it for some homemade pastrami."

And for a taste of the real thing, you might think about going to Syracuse, New York, where Liehs & Steigerwalds meat markets have been making traditional corned beef since 1936. A local blog quotes co-owner Chuck Madonna as saying that prepackaged corned beef is often made by injecting brine into the meat, which both speeds up the process and adds water weight to the cost of the final product. Liehs & Stiegerwalds instead brine theirs for up to three weeks and have thousands of loyal fans.

Grass-Fed Beef. It's Raised Differently. Do You Cook It Differently?

From award-winning cookbook author Jean Anderson,
who is also in the James Beard Cookbook Hall of Fame

Since grass-fed beef is leaner than grain-fed, is there more risk that it will come out drier? Do you need to add more liquid? More fat? Should you cook it for less time?

I asked Chef Sara Moulton, who told me to ask her friend and colleague, Jean Anderson. It turns out that Jean is not only an award-winning cookbook author; she got her degree at Cornell in food chemistry/research. She also studied meat cutting there.

Jean told me, "It's not necessary to increase the amount of liquid when braising grass-fed brisket as long as there's enough NOT TO BOIL DRY. Traditionally, braising calls for very little liquid—add more and you'll be stewing the meat. If the brisket seems unusually lean with little outer covering of fat, I would drape it with slices of bacon, if the bacon is compatible with the particular recipe." (Note: Probably not with the seitan brisket!) Ms. Anderson suggests the usual tightly covered pot and an oven temperature of 300° to 325°F.

She also shared her class notes. "One of the first things we learned in our meat-cutting class is that tender cuts of meat—those cut from the rib or loin or tenderloin—will never be more tender than they are RAW and that the whole aim in cooking them is to preserve as much of the original tenderness as possible (i.e., as fast as possible at high heat with the meat rare, rare, rare)."

And, of course, the corollary: "Tough, sinewy cuts come from the most well-exercised parts of the animal—shank, shoulder, tail, brisket, rump, etc.—and are exactly the reverse, and must be cooked long, low, and slow if they are to become tender."

Lipton Onion Soup Mix

(aka Lipton Recipe Secrets: Golden Onion Recipe Soup & Dip Mix)

(Pssst . . . here's my recipe secret: I use this in my own brisket. So does Ree Drummond!)

What do the pros think about people using Lipton Onion Soup Mix or other packaged ingredients?

Chris Kimball, founder, editor, and president of *Cook's Illustrated*
Me: "What's your sense of packaged ingredients for making a brisket?"

Chris: "Shoot me. Why would you do that? There's only a few ingredients anyway. How long does it take to cut up a couple of onions? You're not saving a lot of time and trouble."

Kenji Lopez-Alt, Managing Editor, Serious Eats
Me: "What about people using Lipton Onion Soup Mix or other packaged ingredients?"

Kenji: "My philosophy is that if you like the way it tastes, stay with it. At the end of the day, you have to like the end result."

Conclusion: Brisket may be pretty forgiving. Chris Kimball . . . not so much.

What's in it, anyway? Let's just say, it's not something you want to share over a jicama salad with Alice Waters.

INGREDIENTS: Onions, Corn Syrup, Cornstarch, Wheat Flour, Salt, Monosodium Glutamate, Partially Hydrogenated, Soybean Oil, Autolyzed Yeast Extract (uh, oh—that sounds especially awful), Chicken Fat, Chicken Powder, Garlic Powder, Natural Flavors, Turmeric, Caramel Color, Parsley, Citric Acid, Torula Yeast, Spices, Disodium Inosinate (huh?)

"So this is where the magic happens."

BRISKET ANXIETY

Le Creuset-ed, Big Green Egg-ed, pink or gray—brisket is what we love. Compared to something like a roast suckling pig stuffed with rice, sausages, apricots, and raisins, this Little Brisket Engine That Could asks for so little. An onion or two. A steady simmer. A gentle rub. A "hey, how're you doin'?" from time to time.

But the road to brisket is paved with good intentions . . . What if we don't do our job? What if we fail it? What if—God forbid—we ruin it? That fear, along with my free-floating anxieties about freezer burn, cellulite, and world peace, is on my permanent worry list.

I asked Kenji Lopez-Alt why a good brisket goes bad. "A surefire way to ruin it," he says, "is to let the meat get above an internal temperature of 180°F. If it reaches 200°F, its juices will be gone. And when it's overcooked, there's no going back." He offers some solace. "You can rescue it—sort of—by shredding the brisket and making a nice bolognese sauce to go on it. Think of it as repurposing it."

> ## "Baste it too much, it dries out. Baste it too little, it dries out."
>
> —*T. J. Burnham, Marlow & Daughters*

I asked him if there were any other challenges. He said, "It's also the size and the lack of fat that makes it difficult. Brisket is flat and wide, which means that it has an extremely high surface area to volume ratio. There's lots of area for moisture to escape, and it's quite easy to overcook. A round pork butt, on the other hand, has a protective layer of rind, is higher in fat, and is pretty round in shape, making it less likely to lose moisture."

If you're a worrier like I am, brisket is a natural. Is the sauce too sweet? Is there too much fat? Am I too fat? Should I have browned it? Who is more trustworthy—Paula Deen or Ree Drummond? Is the timer broken? How is my surface to volume ratio area? And how will I know if I really should worry? A nonplussed blogger relates this story: "Mom was a little distracted when copy/pasting her brisket recipe for me years ago and caught the beginning of a cookie recipe too. So ginger and baking soda went right in with the rest of the ingredients on the list . . . Let's just say one of the other ingredients was vinegar. Things got a little foamy there for a while . . . oddly, still didn't taste bad, I don't know if there is any way to screw up a brisket, it all works for me . . ." Few of us have this low-key, whatever attitude. I believe that there are, with all due respect to Elisabeth Kübler-Ross, five stages of brisket anxiety: Hope, Fear, Panic, Reassurance, Bliss.

If only we all had the confidence of a food blogger who put the following into the headnotes of her brisket recipe: "I'm providing measurements, but when I make it, I never measure anything. I guess I'm rebelling after my tight-ass years as a measure-happy pastry chef." If you do find yourself mired somewhere between Fear and Panic, here's the e-mail address of my good friend Phyllis Cohen, a top psychotherapist, who will be happy to talk you down from the ledge (plcohencsw@aol.com). She also makes a mean brisket. Caution: Only use in case of emergencies.

Finally, for when we delight our guests with a deeply savory, fully satisfying brisket that's bathed in a dense sauce, its rich, steamy aroma delighting all the senses, here is this lovely quote from Hugh Fearnley-Whittingstall's *The River Cottage Meat Book*: "For slow cooking is also the art of making something sublime and special out of something cheap and ordinary."

A wonderful smoky flavor and falling-apart tender, this slow-cooked brisket comes from Chef John Besh. His trick? Starting it on the smoker and finishing in the oven. Recipe p.120.

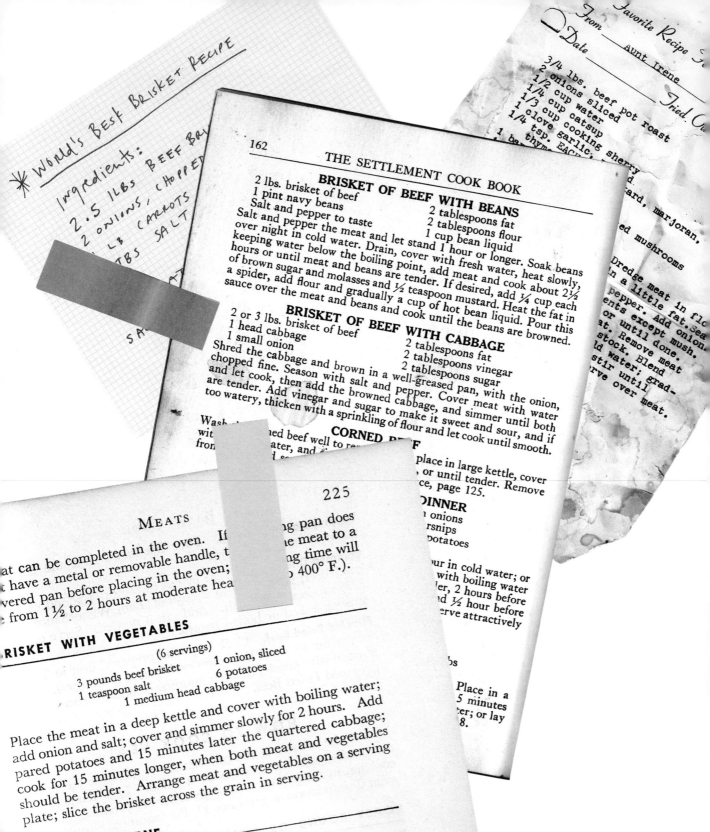

* World's Best Brisket Recipe

Ingredients:
2.5 lbs. Beef Bris...
2 onions, chopped...
lb. carrots
TBS salt
salt

BRISKET OF BEEF WITH BEANS

2 lbs. brisket of beef
1 pint navy beans
Salt and pepper to taste

2 tablespoons fat
2 tablespoons flour
1 cup bean liquid

Salt and pepper the meat and let stand 1 hour or longer. Soak beans over night in cold water. Drain, cover with fresh water, heat slowly, keeping water below the boiling point, add meat and beans cook about 2½ hours or until meat and beans are tender. If desired, add ¼ cup each of brown sugar and molasses and ½ teaspoon mustard. Heat the fat in a spider, add flour and gradually a cup of hot bean liquid. Pour this sauce over the meat and beans and cook until the beans are browned.

BRISKET OF BEEF WITH CABBAGE

2 or 3 lbs. brisket of beef
1 head cabbage
1 small onion

2 tablespoons fat
2 tablespoons vinegar
2 tablespoons sugar

Shred the cabbage and brown in a well-greased pan, with the onion, chopped fine. Season with salt and pepper. Cover meat with water and let cook, then add the browned cabbage, and simmer until both are tender. Add vinegar and sugar to make it sweet and sour, and if too watery, thicken with a sprinkling of flour and let cook until smooth.

CORNED BE...

Wash ...ned beef well to re...
wit... ...ater, and ...
fro... ...d s...

...place in large kettle, cover
..., or until tender. Remove
...ce, page 125.

...DINNER
...n onions
...rsnips
...potatoes

...ur in cold water; or
...with boiling water
...er, 2 hours before
...d ½ hour before
...rve attractively

...at can be completed in the oven. If ...ng pan does
...t have a metal or removable handle, t... ...ng time will
...vered pan before placing in the oven; ... ...o 400° F.).
...e from 1½ to 2 hours at moderate hea...

...RISKET WITH VEGETABLES

(6 servings)

3 pounds beef brisket
1 teaspoon salt
1 medium head cabbage

1 onion, sliced
6 potatoes

Place the meat in a deep kettle and cover with boiling water; add onion and salt; cover and simmer slowly for 2 hours. Add pared potatoes and 15 minutes later the quartered cabbage; cook for 15 minutes longer, when both meat and vegetables should be tender. Arrange meat and vegetables on a serving plate; slice the brisket across the grain in serving.

CHILE CON CARNE

(4 servings)

2 tablespoons fat
...on sliced

Favorite Recipe ...
From
Date   Aunt Irene
      Tried ...

3/4 lbs. beef pot roast
2 onions sliced
1/2 cup water
1/4 cup catsup
1/3 cup cooking sherry
1 clove garlic,
1/4 tsp. thyme, EACH

...ard, marjoran,

...ed mushrooms

Dredge meat in flo...
...n a little fat. Se...
...pepper. Add onion.
...ents except mush.
... or until done.
...at. Remove meat
...stock. Blend
...ld water; grad-
...stir until
...rve over meat.

5 Do I Have a Brisket Recipe for You!

"Some people are infatuated with *Dancing With the Stars*; I'm in love with my grandma's brisket. Funny how things work out."

—*blogs.browardpalmbeach.com*

When I began researching the best home-cooked brisket recipes, I wondered if people would respond. And if they did have a family recipe, would they share their prized family recipes with me? And would they let me put it in a book? Here are the answers: YES! YES! AND YES!

And after the enthusiastic "YES!" and the requisite recipe testing, I would hear something like, "Oh my God, wait 'til I tell my mother that you're using our recipe! She won't believe it! Can you call her and tell her? She's home right now!" Could anything be more heartwarming? Yes, it could: the recipes in this chapter.

Thank you, Roberta Greenberg, for a charmer of a recipe that features Valentine red cranberry slices and is a piquant love letter to brisket. Thank you to Dan and Abby Palmer, for knowing how important it is not to tinker with a classic family recipe. And what good brisket karma they will receive by sharing it with the world! Thanks to Meira Goldberg whose family recipe started in a Hadassah cookbook in Canada and then traveled with Meira to Spain in the '80s, where she served it to her flamenco dancer friends, her Japanese roommate, and her transvestite prostitute neighbor.

Home-cooked briskets are at home all over the world. Devra Ferst, on forward.com, writes about a fourth cousin who served her a brisket in Sweden that Ms. Ferst instantly remembered first eating at her late grandmother's house in Philadelphia. She marvels that this family recipe "had spanned the Atlantic and made its way from Latvia to the United States around the turn of the twentieth century, and to Sweden (by way of Germany) in the 1930s."

"Do you have a brisket recipe?"

Are any or all of these truly "traditional" briskets? It's hard to know these days when Sam's Club touts a "traditional brisket smothered in Italian Barbecue Sauce." The site Post Punk Kitchen gives a recipe for a Blueberry Chipotle Barbecue Sauce that sounds like it's hoping to meet a postmodern barbecued brisket. Fresh, Saucy, and Sweet seeks Tender Hunk. When I raised the question of tradition in a forum called Talk on Serious Eats, I got this reply: "To me, traditional is Lipton's onion soup." (To be fair, this respondent goes on to say that one of her grandmothers "made it the traditional Jewish way—tzimmes, brisket slow cooked with carrots and prunes . . ." and adds, "so for me, savory or sweet is fine.")

Certainly some of the recipes in this chapter have more history than others. Jenny at the Nourished Kitchen—one of the most ardent advocates for healthy, real food—kindly shares her recipe for a classic braised brisket served with tzimmes. She notes that the sweet potato, carrot, and prunes are a traditional Ashkenazic combination, adding a naturally sweet flavor. And her recipe, true to her beliefs, is the only recipe in this book that calls for grass-fed meat. Meira Goldberg's cholent is every bit as authentic. Author Joan Nathan, in *Jewish Cooking in America*, says that her Sabbath stew "is one of those dishes that has distinguished Jewish cooks since at least the fourth century." Sauerkraut (pickled shredded cabbage) also goes back centuries. Gil Marks, in the *Encyclopedia of Jewish Food*, notes that the technique dates back more than twenty-four hundred years to China and was first introduced to Eastern Europe around the sixteenth century—quite a few years before it was introduced to hot dogs and mustard. So there is "traditional" and there is "traditional." I think the rule of thumb might be that it couldn't be from the Old World if it is made with Diet Dr Pepper in the New World.

Of course, tradition isn't just about what's served. It's also about where it's served. People who want great huge plates of juicy barbecue on white bread have always been happy to go out and get it—in restaurants, rib shacks, barbecue joints; from local food trucks; at cook-offs and competitions. Generally, barbecue lovers are happy to leave the arduous smoking to the pros.

I've got the best brisket recipe ever!'"

A braised brisket, on the other hand, is pretty much always served at home. Looking more Uggs than Manolo (chunks of dark brown meat lying in a pool of dark brown sauce with a side of plain buttered noodles), this sturdy entrée is not the colorful culinary tour de force that has restaurant diners whipping out their iPhones to shoot. At the few upscale restaurants that do have braised brisket on their menus (some only for Jewish holidays), the chefs I spoke to told me that the presentation had to be very very polished—i.e., brisket that is cut into precise and elegant squares. (Todd Gray's at Equinox is one.) It could be a brisket with a single note and fresh appeal, like the brisket recipe I received from Baltimore chef John Shields that calls for plump, ripe summer peaches. It's not on any restaurant menu that I know of, but another beauty is the early spring brisket from Molly Stevens (it's in her book *All About Braising*) with fresh rhubarb and honey.

There are some emotional components that make a brisket feel traditional, authentic, homemade. Love and familiarity, of course. You're not serving it to strangers, restaurant critics, or snarky Yelp-ers.

Tolerance is part of it. From a young woman in Portland, Maine, who wishes to remain anonymous: "My grandmother's brisket recipe wasn't good. It was made with love but it was missing flavor. We ate it anyway."

Kindness factors in, too. Over and over, I met people who would share their family's recipe. Especially with someone like me whose mother never made a brisket. And they wouldn't even ask how that was possible. Their kindness extended to sharing their recipes online with total strangers. Of course, not everyone shares everything. "My mother would cover in onions, carrots, and a little water (plus bay leaf, salt, pepper, etc.), braise it, then chill, defat, and slice . . . can't give you exact measurements, it is apparently forbidden (see page 273 of the Talmud)," says a wry Chowhound post. And I have a friend (let's call her

Brisket Loves Ketchup

You can never be too rich or too thick. Which is why ketchup is the main squeeze in most barbecue sauces and many braised briskets. Perfect Heinz is the gold standard but if you are using grass-fed meat for your brisket, you might want to consider Organicville Organic Ketchup.

"Rose") who would rather not share her grandmother's much-swooned-over recipe. When seriously pressed, "Rose" does give the recipe to someone. She just leaves out one of the essential ingredients.

What else goes into homemade briskets besides love, forgiveness, a willingness to share, and a tiny pinch of duplicity? Pride. That's what struck me most when I spoke to the brisket cooks, their mothers, uncles, great-aunts, cousins, brothers-in-law. They all bask in the heady mix of family history, memories, continuity, ritual, in the belief that it gets better with every bite and every generation. They're proud of everything, from their antique silver serving spoon to the technique they use to peel the tiny pearl onions.

And there is more than a little ego involved. I asked my therapist friend, Phyllis Cohen (I gave you her e-mail address in Chapter 4), why everyone who proudly announces, "I've got the perfect brisket recipe ever!" isn't kidding. Phyllis suggests that "with some food, there's a right way and a wrong way. With brisket there's only 'my way.'"

I put the same question to the extremely modest chef and pit master Brian Perrone of Slows in Detroit.

ME: "Why do you think everyone says they have the best brisket recipe?"

BRIAN: "Whoever's making it is right."

PAUSE.

BRIAN: "I like mine more than others."

"I'm plotzing here. Ketchup? Cans of soup? OY!!"

—Chowhound

Which is why I wasn't totally surprised to hear about an annual Bring Your Best Brisket party held every year at Chanukah by one competitive brisket-loving family. Melissa Bachrach, a home cook from Pacific Palisades, California, told me it was first started by her cousin's non-Jewish wife. It's a tough crowd: everything from richly complex, gently seasoned boeuf daubes to silken home-smoked deli-style brisket recipes have been entered. This past year Melissa was proud that she had won by a landslide. Unfortunately, it wasn't for her mother's recipe ("I can't bring my mother's brisket because it didn't win the first time"), but for an online recipe by Deb Perelman, founder of smitten kitchen, who is super proud of Melissa.

A Partial List of Brisket's Sometimes Surprising Ingredients

Campbell's Beef Consommé	Stout	Gingerbread
Ginger ale	Belgian beer	Pineapple juice
Franco-American Slow Roast Beef Gravy	Dr Pepper	Orange juice
Miso	Licorice root	Lemons
Lipton's Onion Soup Mix	Beef suet	Peaches
Coffee	Gingersnaps	Tahini sauce
Soy sauce	Mole sauce	Sauce Arturo
Pomegranate juice	Korean ground red chile	Gold's duck sauce (kosher for Passover)
Apple juice	Emeril's Essence Creole Seasoning	Root beer
Decaffeinated coffee	Strips of ham	Aleppo pepper
Jellied cranberry sauce	Liquid Smoke	
Coca-Cola	Powdered mace	

For fun, I posed this question online: What shouldn't go into a brisket? One of the best responses was "Strawberry Quik." The other was "chicken." Brisket people are like that.

MY FORMER BEST FRİEND'S EX-MOTHER-İN-LAW'S BRİSKET

Adapted from the author's recipe

Serves 6–8

If you love your brisket bathed in a sweet, rich, thick tomatoey sauce, this is for you. When I got this recipe, I had never made a brisket before. And suddenly, I was a star. This takes next to no prep time, uses simple ingredients, and always gets raves. I add fresh carrots for sweetness, texture, and to assuage my guilt about using so many packaged ingredients. Tiny tips: The foil just adds an extra seal. And if the sauce is too thin at the end, just reduce it in a pan on top of the stove.

2	tablespoons vegetable oil
1	(3- to 4-pound) beef brisket, trimmed
1	cup red wine (something big and rich, like a Malbec)
1	cup Heinz chili sauce
1	cup Heinz ketchup
1	envelope Lipton dry golden onion soup mix
4	large carrots, peeled, trimmed, and sliced on the bias into 1-inch pieces
	Handful of chopped fresh Italian parsley leaves

Preheat the oven to 325°F.

In a large heavy skillet, heat the oil over medium-high heat until hot. Add the brisket and brown on both sides, 5 to 7 minutes per side. Transfer the brisket to a platter and set aside. In a bowl, combine the wine, chili sauce, ketchup, and 1 cup of water and set aside.

Line an ovenproof enameled cast-iron pot or other heavy pot with a tight-fitting lid, just large enough to hold the brisket snugly, with heavy-duty aluminum foil, leaving enough overhang to seal over the brisket. Sprinkle half of the soup mix on the bottom of the foil, then top with the brisket. Sprinkle the remaining soup mix on top of the brisket. Pour the reserved liquid mixture on top of the brisket. Place the carrots around the brisket, making sure they are covered with the sauce. Sprinkle the parsley over everything.

Tightly seal the foil, encasing the brisket and all the other ingredients inside the packet. Cover the pot, then place in the oven and braise until fork-tender, about 3½ hours. Transfer the brisket to a cutting board and slice the meat against the grain to the desired thickness. Serve with the sauce and carrots.

TEMPLE EMANU-EL BRISKET

Serves 8–10

Quivering cranberry slices that melt into the meat and slowly caramelize give this brisket its lovely character. Even better, it takes so little effort for this sweet alchemy to work. Roberta Greenberg, the long-time assistant to the rabbis at this well-known New York City synagogue and the keeper of this recipe, suggests reducing the sauce on the stove after reheating it if you prefer it thicker. It is good enough to make you convert.

1   (4- to 5-pound) beef brisket

2   teaspoons garlic powder

1   teaspoon paprika

    Kosher salt and freshly ground black pepper

4   large onions, peeled and cut into eighths

2   (14-ounce) cans jellied cranberry sauce, sliced

All recipes come with permission. This one comes with a blessing. I had begged both Ms. Greenberg and Rabbi Posner for this recipe, which I found on Temple Emanu-El's Web site. Surely they couldn't keep it to themselves—I couldn't imagine the book without it. Ms. Greenberg properly asked me to check with the head rabbi, David M. Posner. Rabbi Posner, every bit as sweet and tender as the brisket recipe itself, made me smile with the following e-mail: "I ran this, of course, by my wife, of 41 years. She said, 'Davey . . . what about my recipe for 'steak continental?' I responded, 'Tzipi . . . please . . . don't get involved . . . I want to keep my job.' You have my permission. Best wishes . . . dmp"

Sprinkle both sides of the brisket with the garlic powder, paprika, and salt and pepper. Tightly cover the brisket with plastic wrap and refrigerate for 2 days.

When you're ready to finish the dish, preheat the oven to 500°F.

Unwrap the brisket, place it in a roasting pan, and roast for 20 minutes on each side. Remove the pan from the oven and decrease the temperature to 350°F. Place the onions under and around the brisket, then cover the top of the meat with the cranberry sauce slices. Tightly cover the pan with heavy-duty aluminum foil and cook until fork-tender, about 3 hours.

Remove the pan from the oven and allow the brisket to cool. Transfer the brisket to a cutting board, trim the fat, then slice the meat against the grain to the desired thickness. Return the slices to the pot, overlapping them at an angle so that you can see a bit of the top edge of each slice, cover the pan with foil, and refrigerate overnight.

The next day, remove any congealed fat from the top of the sauce. Heat the brisket, covered, at 350°F for 20 minutes, then, uncovered, for another 20 to 30 minutes, until hot and the sauce has reduced a bit. Serve with the sauce.

AUNT GLADYS'S BRISKET

Serves 8

This classic is adapted from a much loved family recipe given to me by Abby Shulman Palmer and Daniel S. Palmer. It's simple and savory—all taste and texture—thanks to the pucker of the sauerkraut and the sweetness of the brown sugar. I must have received twenty recipes with sauerkraut as an ingredient and this one was the winner, hands down.

2	tablespoons vegetable oil
1	(4-pound) beef brisket, trimmed
1	onion, diced
1	(27-ounce) can sauerkraut (with juice)
1	(28-ounce) can diced tomatoes
½	teaspoon salt
½	cup brown sugar

One or two days before you plan to serve the brisket, heat the oil in an ovenproof enameled cast-iron pot or other heavy pot with a tight-fitting lid just large enough to hold the brisket snugly over medium-high heat until hot. Add the brisket and brown well on both sides, 5 to 7 minutes per side. Place the onion, sauerkraut, and tomatoes on top of and around the brisket, then sprinkle with the salt. Cover, bring to a boil, then simmer gently on top of the stove for 45 minutes.

In a small bowl, combine the brown sugar with some cooking liquid from the pot, then pour the sugar mixture over the brisket. Continue to simmer gently, covered, until fork-tender, 1½ to 2 hours. Turn the brisket over a couple of times while simmering, spooning some sauerkraut and liquid on top of the brisket each time. If there isn't enough liquid, just add some water.

Transfer the brisket to a cutting board, allow it to cool slightly, then slice it against the grain. Place the slices in an oven-safe baking dish, overlapping them at an angle so that you can see a bit of the top edge of each slice. Spoon the sauerkraut mixture and sauce over the meat, cover the dish with aluminum foil, and refrigerate for up to 2 days. (The dish may also be frozen.)

When ready to serve, preheat the oven to 350°F. Bring the brisket to room temperature, then bake, covered, until the meat is hot and the sauce is bubbling, 35 to 45 minutes. Check the seasonings, then serve immediately.

GRANDMA RUBY'S CHOLENT

Serves 8–10

From Meira Goldberg and adapted from a Canadian Hadassah cookbook, this calls for cubes of brisket, so it is really a stew. It is—as a proper cholent should be—a hearty meal in one: simple, substantial, filling. You can use short ribs in place of the brisket and substitute fava beans, red beans, or black beans for the navy beans.

1	tablespoon all-purpose flour
2	teaspoons kosher salt
2	teaspoons paprika
½	teaspoon freshly ground black pepper
1	(3-pound) beef brisket, trimmed and cut into 2-inch cubes
3	tablespoons olive oil
3	onions, peeled and sliced
3	cloves garlic, minced
2	cups navy beans, picked over, rinsed, soaked overnight, and drained
¾	cup pearl barley, rinsed
6	medium baking potatoes, peeled and quartered

Preheat the oven to 250°F.

In a small bowl, combine the flour, salt, paprika, and pepper, then dust the brisket with the mixture. In a large, heavy skillet, heat the oil over medium-high heat until hot. Add the meat in batches, if necessary, and brown on all sides. Remove the meat with a slotted spoon and place in a large ovenproof enameled cast-iron pot or other heavy pot with a tight-fitting lid and set aside.

Reduce the heat to medium and add the onions. Cook, stirring occasionally, until caramelized, 15 to 20 minutes. Add the garlic and cook, stirring occasionally, for about 1 minute. Add some water and deglaze the pan, scraping up the browned bits with a wooden spoon. Add the onions, garlic, and liquid to the pot, followed by the navy beans, pearl barley, and potatoes. Cover the ingredients with water, stir to combine, and bring the liquid to a boil over high heat.

Cover the pot, then bake in the oven for about 12 hours, or until the meat is tender and the sauce is thick and rich. Check the pot occasionally and add more water to cover, if necessary. Do not stir the mixture, though, or the potatoes will break up. Skim any fat from the surface and adjust the seasonings before slicing against the grain and serving.

BRAISED BRISKET WITH TZIMMES

Serves 8–10

Adapted from nourishedkitchen.com, this transcendent Rosh Hashanah brisket is bursting with robust good health and rich, sublime flavor. No pop-it-in-the-oven quickie, it is well worth the considerable effort. Grass-fed beef is bathed in tangy hard apple cider and homemade stock, then sweet potatoes, carrots, and prunes–a traditional Ashkenazic dish called tzimmes–are added. Pan juices combine with more cider for a mildly sweet, smooth reduction sauce.

BRISKET

2 to 3 tablespoons grass-fed beef tallow (see Notes)

1 (4- to 5-pound) beef brisket, preferably grass-fed, trimmed

1 quart beef stock, preferably homemade

1 pint hard cider (see Notes)

REDUCTION SAUCE

2 tablespoons grass-fed beef tallow (see Notes)

2 shallots, peeled and thinly sliced

1 cup hard cider

TZIMMES

6 large carrots, peeled and chopped into bite-size coins

3 large sweet potatoes or garnet yams, peeled and chopped into bite-size pieces

2 cups pitted prunes

Preheat the oven to 300°F.

For the brisket, heat the tallow in a large skillet or griddle until it melts and becomes quite hot. Sear the brisket on each side, 3 to 4 minutes, then place it in a large clay baker, pouring the stock and cider over the brisket. Braise the brisket, covered, for 3 hours before preparing the tzimmes.

For the tzimmes, after the brisket has cooked for 3 hours, add the carrots and sweet potatoes or yams to the clay baker. Cook for another hour. Add the prunes to the clay baker, increase the heat to 375°F, and continue to cook for 30 to 45 minutes.

Remove the brisket to a serving dish to rest and scoop up the tzimmes with a slotted spoon, placing them around the brisket. Strain the liquid from the clay baker into a container, remove any fat, and set the liquid aside. Keep the brisket and tzimmes warm in your oven with the heat turned off while you prepare the reduction sauce.

For the reduction sauce, in a large saucepan, melt the beef tallow over medium heat, then add the shallots and cook, stirring occasionally. When the shallots release their fragrance and begin to caramelize a bit, add the reserved liquid and the hard cider. Simmer slowly until the liquids are reduced by half. Adjust the seasonings. Slice the brisket against the grain and serve with the tzimmes and the sauce.

NOTES FROM JENNY AT NOURISHEDKITCHEN.COM:

This calls for grass-fed beef tallow. Get it online or substitute another fat: unrefined palm oil, if you're keeping the dish kosher; pastured bacon fat, grass-fed butter, or ghee, if you're not.

You can substitute plain apple cider or juice for the hard cider. If you do, the brisket and reduction sauce will be sweeter.

If you don't have a clay baker, use an ovenproof enameled cast-iron pot or other heavy pot with a tight-fitting lid, just large enough to hold the meat snugly.

"This transcendent Rosh Hashanah brisket is bursting with robust good health and rich, sublime flavor."

—*Nourishedkitchen.com*

MY MOTHER'S BRISKET

Adapted from Gourmet, December 1995

Serves 10–12

A truly delectable brisket, this has the distinction of being the only recipe in this book where the lid on the baking pan is left ajar. If you prefer a richer sauce, substitute half beef broth and half wine for the water. Tip: It's really important for the flavor and the color of the finished sauce to slowly cook the onions until deep golden.

3   tablespoons vegetable oil

1   (5- to 6-pound) first-cut beef brisket

¾   teaspoon salt

¾   teaspoon freshly ground black pepper

3   large yellow onions, cut into ½-inch pieces

2 or 3 large cloves garlic, or to taste, minced

1   teaspoon paprika, preferably Hungarian

Preheat the oven to 375°F.

In a Dutch oven or other heavy baking pan large enough to hold the brisket, heat 1 tablespoon of the oil in the oven for 10 minutes. Pat the brisket dry and season with salt and pepper to taste. Roast the brisket in the pan, uncovered, for 30 minutes.

While the brisket is roasting, in a large heavy skillet cook the onions in the remaining 2 tablespoons of oil over moderately high heat, stirring, until softened and beginning to turn golden. Reduce the heat and cook the onions, stirring occasionally and reducing the heat if necessary, until deep golden, about 20 minutes more. Stir in the garlic, paprika, salt, and pepper and cook for 1 minute. Stir in 3 cups of water and bring to a boil.

Spoon the onion mixture over the brisket and bake, covered, with lid ½ inch ajar, until the brisket is fork-tender, about 3½ hours. (Check the pan every hour; if necessary, add more water.) Remove the brisket from the oven and cool in the onion mixture for 1 hour.

Remove the brisket from the pan, scraping the onion mixture back into the pan, and chill, wrapped in aluminum foil, overnight. Spoon the onion mixture into a 1-quart measuring cup and chill, covered, overnight.

Preheat the oven to 350°F.

Discard the fat from the onion mixture, add enough water to the mixture to measure 3 cups total, if necessary, and in a blender blend the gravy until smooth. Trim the fat, then slice the brisket against the grain (thick or thin). In a large ovenproof skillet heat the gravy until hot, add the brisket, cover with foil, and heat in the oven for about 30 minutes.

SLOW COOKER BRISKET

Serves 8

Relax. Let the ingredients do all the work in this warm, welcoming dish. The beer tenderizes the meat, the onion soup gives it sweetness and depth, the chili sauce goes "zing!" This is from Tammie Barker, who notes that the same basic recipe can be used for up to seven pounds of brisket if your slow cooker can handle that much. True to her hometown, she uses a local beer in it (Boulevard Brewing Co.'s Pale Ale), and serves it with a Kansas City sauce (Fiorella's Jack Stack Barbecue KC Original).

6   ounces beer

1   envelope onion soup mix

12   ounces chili sauce, such as Heinz

1   (4-pound) beef brisket, trimmed

In a slow cooker with a minimum 3½-quart capacity, combine the beer, soup mix, and chili sauce. Add the brisket and coat with the sauce. (Note that in the smaller models, the meat may not lie flat.) Cover the cooker and cook on low until the brisket is fork-tender, 8 to 10 hours.

Transfer the brisket to a cutting board and slice against the grain. If the sauce needs to be thickened and intensified, reduce it in a pan on the stove before serving with the brisket.

If You Don't Say So Yourself

Everyone seems to think they have THE definitive brisket recipe. A partial list of inspired recipe titles I've come across:

Chef Dean's Never-Fail Brisket

Kbell's Perfect Brisket

Best Ever Brisket Recipe

The Greatest Brisket Ever Recipe

Best (Non-BBQ) Beef Brisket Sandwich Ever

Dad's Best Brisket Recipe

My Best Beef Brisket Recipe

The Most Incredible BBQ Beef Brisket Sandwich on the Face of the Planet!

My Perfect Slow-Smoked Brisket Method

Simple, Perfect Fresh-Ground Brisket Burgers Recipe

Best Beef Brisket Crock-Pot Recipe

Jewish Grandma's Best Beef Brisket Recipe

The Best Brisket in the World

Best Barbecue Hickory-Smoked Brisket

World-Champion Brisket

Best Brisket Ever!!!!!!

Barbecue Beef Brisket That Doesn't Suck

6 Me. Joan Nathan. A Brisket.

"To me, brisket is the Zelig of meats."

—Joan Nathan, author, doyenne of Jewish cooking

Me. Nach Waxman. A Brisket.

"Looking for the original recipe for brisket is like looking for the original recipe for toast."

—Nach Waxman, founder, Kitchen Arts & Letters

If a traditional Jewish brisket recipe is not in your family, borrow Joan's or Nach's. Joan and Nach are two of the most iconic names in the culinary world and like "Julia" and "Marcella," we're all on a first-name basis. Early on in the brisket-making portion of my quest, I realized that it's almost impossible for someone to say the name "Joan Nathan" without reflexively adding "the doyenne of Jewish cooking." And when you talk about Nach Waxman, warm hugs and huzzahs abound. "Nach Waxman is the alpha and omega of the recorded history of food," says Eat Me Daily. No one has ever—well, at least not yet—said that about me.

What have Joan and Nach done to deserve this? And what did I have to do to deserve a stint in each of their kitchens, watching them make their favorite brisket? You mean, besides begging, cajoling, wheedling, and obsessively e-mailing them until they could hold out no longer? That's exactly what I did; I couldn't imagine this book without their briskets. Each recipe debuted inside the family and has been passed down for years, starred in cookbooks, and comes up within seconds when you Google "braised brisket recipes."

I believe that Joan and Nach are astral twins, born under the sign of Brisket. They share an intellectual curiosity about culinary culture and history. Each has a passion for furthering the ever-evolving community of food, encouraging cooks to value what's real, make what they love, and share what they make. And they both grew up in brisket families. Each has a mother (in Nach's case, a mother-in-law, too) who passed down the secrets for a superb never-fail brisket.

Ms. Nathan is a food historian, the author of ten cookbooks, and a regular contributor to the *New York Times*. Her much-acclaimed *Jewish Cooking in America* won both the James Beard Award and the IACP/Julia Child Cookbook of the Year Award. The PBS television series that followed was as lavishly praised. Nach Waxman—who is also a large presence in this book—is the president of Kitchen Arts & Letters, the only culinary bookstore in Manhattan. The *New York Times* calls

"I believe that Joan and Nach are astral twins, born under the sign of Brisket."

Mr. Waxman "the most sought-after expert on food history and publishing in New York." I would add, in the country. His customers/fans include an international array of cooks, restaurant owners, caterers, cooking teachers, food writers, editors, chefs, and chefs who send their most promising prep cooks to the store in order to broaden their worldview. I can't name names because KA&L doesn't name names.

And while Nach has over 12,000 titles in the store at any given time, he is a passionate advocate for not cooking with recipes. His hope is that people will get to know and appreciate food on a much more visceral level—understanding the ingredients that go into a dish, learning what and why flavors go together, and then internalizing this knowledge.

BRISKETING WITH JOAN NATHAN

My day with Joan—who lives in a sunny, sprawling white house in a leafy suburb of Washington, D.C.—was a revelation. Joan is so relaxed in her kitchen that you immediately think, oh, it's that easy? I don't have to be all teaspoony and micro-measured, counting out the peppercorns? Joan's kitchen, by the way, is probably twice as large as my whole apartment. It has vast counter space; a long, lovely country dining table; well-used pots and pans; cookbooks and fresh flowers. It's a homey home for a cook who is not the least bit fussy or pretentious.

Joan prepped for my visit with a huge brisket flat, a sturdy four-pounder that she had had the butcher trim of some fat. Carrots, onions, celery, and sprigs of herbs surrounded this hunky meat, suggesting a colorful still life that could have been painted in the 1700s.

Throughout the prepping and the cooking, I asked Joan questions. Joan, you should know, is the ultimate multi-multitasker. At any given time during our brisket session, two phones would ring, six e-mails would come in, the plumber would have an urgent question about the drip in the ceiling, Joan's assistant would need an okay for a speaking engagement, Joan would be discussing lunch (no brisket yet—it had hours to go), Joan would be looking for a wine opener, and the director for my book video would be waving Joan closer to the stove so we could get a shot of the brisket browning. And she didn't miss a beat.

ME: "What makes a Jewish brisket so special?"

JOAN: "The love. Brisket is such comfort food. Smell my house."

ME: "I think there should be a brisket fragrance—eau de brisket."

ME, THINKING: "Could they spritz it at Bloomingdale's? Hmm . . ."

ME: "What makes your recipe so special to you?"

JOAN: "Everyone grew up with their mother's brisket and so did I. My mother made a kind
of sauerbraten. She served it many times throughout the year, especially for Rosh
Hashanah and Chanukah, with farfel, tiny bits of tiny noodles, like tiny Israeli couscous.
She still makes it although she is a mere ninety-seven years old."

ME: "Brisket basics?"

JOAN: "When you make it, get a first cut with some fat on it. There's nothing worse than a
dry brisket."

ME: "Slice before or after cooking?"

JOAN: "After, with slices about ¼ inch thick."

ME: "To freeze or not? The leftovers, I mean."

JOAN: "Freeze always. No problem."

Me: "If you're Jewish and you make a terrible
brisket, does that make you a bad person?"

Joan: "It just means you probably don't
put in enough water for a good braise."

"My mother, who taught me this recipe."

Left: "My mother and father, Pearl and Ernest Nathan, me, my brother Alan."
Right: "Three generations: me, my mother, and my children, Daniela, David, and Merissa."

JOAN, PUTTING HER BRISKET IN THE OVEN: "You can never have too much brisket."

ME: Sigh.

Joan leaves to answer the door. After Joan browns the behemoth (why does her brisket look like it's getting BIGGER as the day goes on?), she plunks it on top of the onions, and douses it generously with canned tomatoes and splashes of red wine. In her vintage Le Creuset, of course. Bright red, of course. As the brisket slowly cooks, it soon fills the house with aromas so intense that even if you weren't hungry, you'd be hungry. One difference, by the way, between Joan's brisket and most others is that she bastes hers while it cooks.

And while we breathe in the blissful aromatic brisket atmosphere, I ask Joan for some specific tips for those of us who haven't written ten cookbooks.

*Joan, prepping her brisket, showing
lots of vegetable love.*

ME: "What if you're pressed for time?"

JOAN: "If you're in a hurry, don't sear the meat before. And while I do sauté onions for my brisket, if you're in a hurry, you can just throw the onions in."

ME: "Any shortcuts?"

JOAN: "I'll cook two briskets at once and freeze one. I do them in two ovens."

ME: "What do you do with leftovers?"

JOAN: "Sometimes I put a little ketchup in with the sauce, mix it with noodles, and have another meal."

ME: "You can't go wrong if . . . ?"

JOAN: "The more onions, the better. Oh, and a little more wine will never hurt."

ME: "You're so relaxed about all this. Any hard-and-fast rules?"

JOAN: "Keep the fat on the meat while you cook it—take it off the brisket after it's cooked and cooled. Prepare the brisket in advance and refrigerate it overnight."

ME, tasting: "It's not possible for something to taste this good."

JOAN, SMILING: "Even if you don't love meat, you love brisket."

MY FAVORITE BRISKET (Not Too Gedempte Fleysch)

Adapted from Jewish Cooking in America, by Joan Nathan, Knopf, 1994

Serves 10

Basically, this is what you'd offer your future in-laws to ensure their undying affection. This is a taste-great, feel-good classic Jewish brisket, but while the recipe has been in the family for years, Joan is not averse to a new tweak or twist: Add a jar of sun-dried tomatoes, dry or packed in oil, for a more intense flavor. Or add a 2-inch knob of ginger and a few large strips of lemon zest to the pot—remove them before serving. Note: "Not Too Gedempte Fleysch" means "Not too well stewed." I didn't know either.

2   teaspoons salt

    Freshly ground black pepper

1   (5-pound) brisket of beef, shoulder roast of beef, chuck roast, or end of steak

1   clove garlic, peeled

2   tablespoons vegetable oil

3   onions, peeled and diced

1   (10-ounce) can tomatoes

2   cups red wine

2   stalks celery with the leaves, chopped

1   bay leaf

1   sprig thyme

1   sprig rosemary

¼   cup chopped parsley

6 to 8 carrots, peeled and sliced on the diagonal

Preheat the oven to 325°F. Sprinkle the salt and pepper to taste over the brisket and rub with the garlic. Sear the brisket in the oil and then place, fat side up, on top of the onions in a large casserole. Cover with the tomatoes, red wine, celery, bay leaf, thyme, and rosemary.

Cover and bake in the oven for about 3 hours, basting often with the pan juices.

Add the parsley and carrots and bake, uncovered, for 30 minutes more, or until the carrots are cooked. To test for doneness, stick a fork in the brisket. When there is a light pull on the fork as it is removed from the meat, it is "fork-tender."

This dish is best prepared in advance and refrigerated so that the fat can be easily skimmed from the surface of the gravy. When ready to serve, preheat the oven to 350°F. Reheat the gravy in a pan on the stove. Some people like to strain the gravy, but Joan prefers to keep the onions because they are so delicious.

Trim off all the visible fat from the cold brisket. Then place the brisket, on what was the fat side down, on a cutting board. Look for the grain—that is, the muscle lines of the brisket—and with a sharp knife, cut across the grain.

Put the sliced brisket in a roasting pan. Pour the hot gravy on the meat, cover, and reheat in the oven for about 30 minutes.

Me, taking a brisket tutorial from the tenured professor of brisket.

Kitchen Arts & Letters, the definitive culinary bookstore.

BRISKETING WITH NACH WAXMAN

Nach and his wife, Maron, live in New York City in a vintage prewar apartment that is filled with art and beloved family treasures and exudes a well lived-in feel. Nach's cooking style feels equally comfortable and without artifice. The well-organized, non-renovated kitchen does not dazzle with the bling of four-inch lava stone counters and there's not a molecular gastronomic device in sight. Nach tells me he and Maron like to stay home and eat. "We eat simply. If you want to dress something up, you don't dress it up by making it more elaborate," he says. "You dress it up by giving it a different taste . . . different flavors." Is there a better place to learn about comfort food?

Nach grew up in a tradition of brisket on New York's Lower East Side. When his mother made brisket, he was an ardent observer. "That's how I learned about cooking. From watching." From his father's side, descendants of Romania, he learned to prefer a savory brisket to a sweet one.

Nach's brisket recipe is an amalgam of his mother's and his mother-in-law's, and a tribute to both of them. Nach gives credit where it is due. "The key element from my mother-in-law was interim slicing. She had this brilliant notion of what would be good—by cutting the meat and putting it back in the pot, you've created more surface area for browning. Interim slicing lets every piece be exposed to heat and juices and allows the flavor to penetrate the entire brisket. If you slice later, it's also going to be less flavorful." (Full disclosure: I'm thinking, "Why didn't I think of interim slicing? Why didn't I think of inventing Post-it notes?")

Left: Nach's mother-in-law, Helen Loeb, with her two daughters.
Right: Nach's mother, Minnie Waxman.

Back to brisket. Nach adds, "I find that the typical unsliced brisket has a beautiful exterior—but inside the meat is gray. By slicing halfway through the cooking and reassembling, every piece essentially gets to be an outside piece. The slices are beautiful; the meat is much firmer and is less likely to either fall apart or shred."

This is a man who knows his brisket. And truly, I am mesmerized. "I take the gravy and spoon it on top when I have reassembled the pieces of meat—each piece gets a rich flavor. It's akin to a basting process—with this technique you are internally basting." Internally basting! Why didn't I invent internal basting?

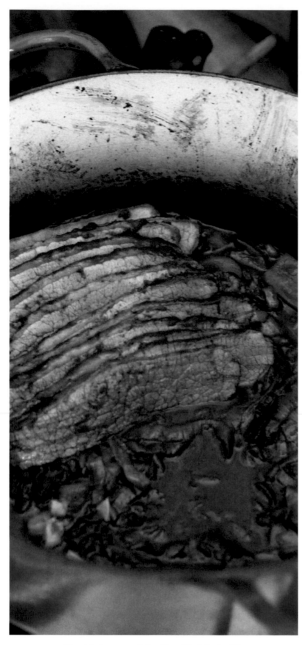

Nach's impeccably sliced brisket with its single carrot. Recipe p. 110.

"The robustly browned slices look like a chorus line of lovely Rockettes, one leaning into the other in perfectly gorgeous symmetry."

The other distinctive feature of Nach's brisket (and this comes from his mother) is that no water is added; all the liquid comes from the meat and from the onions. (You'll see, in the recipe that follows, that you can add a little water if you ABSOLUTELY have to.)

While I am watching the "you-can-tell-he's-done-this-before" browning and cooking ("This is my Equinox," Nach says, referring to his neighborhood gym, as he lifts the über-heavyweight Le Creuset when he puts it in and then takes it out of the oven.) I get to see how his slicing technique works and watch how easy it is for him to re-compose the brisket. With the brisket happily simmering, I ask Nach for the brisket rules he lives by.

Nach Waxman's School of Better Briskets:

- "Avoid the temptation to add water."

- "Browning is crucial for taste. You want a nice crisp brown on the meat."

- "You can't use enough onions (when you're cooking them, scrape up the crispy particles in the pan,which will make the onions brown in a way they never would otherwise. And keep the heat kind of high while browning.)"

- "It is better the next day; not only does it freeze well, it actually improves with freezing."

- "Reheating should not be tightly covered; rather, fit some foil loosely over whatever vessel you heat it in."

- "Use black pepper liberally."

At one point during the cooking session, Nach modestly confides, "I don't think I'm a great cook. I'm an attentive home cook." When his brisket—with few ingredients and an abundance of superb technique—is done, every pampered slice is richly caramelized and liberally sauced; deep primal flavor and heavenly aromas delight all the senses.

Hey, Nach—you're a great cook!

Everything knows its place in Nach's well-organized kitchen.

NACH WAXMAN'S BRISKET OF BEEF

Adapted from The New Basics Cookbook by Julee Rosso and Sheila Lukins, Workman, 1989

Serves 10–12

This is the go-to recipe for knowledgeable brisket lovers. Who then share it with others. Who share it with—perhaps—the Obamas and other notable families. So warm and welcoming, the secret is what Nach did way before anyone else: slice the meat midway through cooking. If you serve this the day after you make it, reheat, covered, for about 1 hour in a 325°F oven.

1 **(6-pound) first-cut beef brisket, trimmed so that a thin layer of fat remains**

   All-purpose flour, for dusting

   Freshly ground black pepper

3 **tablespoons corn oil**

8 **medium onions, peeled and thickly sliced**

3 **tablespoons tomato paste**

   Kosher salt

2 to 4 **cloves garlic, peeled and quartered**

1 **carrot, peeled and trimmed**

Preheat the oven to 375°F.

Lightly dust the brisket with flour, then sprinkle with pepper to taste. Heat the oil over medium-high heat in a large ovenproof enameled cast-iron pot or other heavy pot with a lid just large enough to hold the brisket snugly. Add the brisket to the pot and brown on both sides until crusty brown areas appear on the surface here and there, 5 to 7 minutes per side. Transfer the brisket to a platter, turn up the heat a bit, then add the onions to the pot and stir constantly with a wooden spoon, scraping up any browned bits stuck to the bottom of the pot. Cook until the onions have softened and developed a rich brown color but aren't yet caramelized, 10 to 15 minutes.

Turn off the heat and place the brisket and any accumulated juices on top of the onions.

Spread the tomato paste over the brisket as if you were icing a cake. Sprinkle with salt and more pepper to taste, then add the garlic and carrot to the pot. Cover the pot, transfer to the oven, and cook the brisket for 1½ hours.

Transfer the brisket to a cutting board and, using a very sharp knife, slice the meat across the grain into approximately ⅛-inch-thick slices. Return the slices to the pot, overlapping them at an angle so that you can see a bit of the top edge of each slice. The end result should resemble the original unsliced brisket leaning slightly backward. Check the seasonings and, if absolutely necessary, add 2 to 3 teaspoons of water to the pot.

Cover the pot and return to the oven. Lower the heat to 325°F and cook the brisket until it is fork-tender, about 2 hours. Check once or twice during cooking to make sure that the liquid is not bubbling away. If it is, add a few more teaspoons of water—but not more. Also, each time you check, spoon some of the liquid on top of the roast so that it drips down between the slices.

It is ready to serve with its juices, but, in fact, it's even better the second day.

The proud father of a beautiful, six-pound brisket!

KNICHES,
UGELS,
and
USCOUS

y Search
r Jewish
Cooking
n France

JOAN
ATHAN

KNOPF

MARKS

ENCYCLOPEDIA OF

JEWISH FOOD

WILEY

Smithsonian
Books

97 ORCHARD

AN EDIBLE HISTORY OF FIVE IMMIGRANT
FAMILIES IN ONE NEW YORK TENEMENT

JANE ZIEGELMAN

HARPER

JOHN
BESH

THE COOKBOOK

My New Orleans

NIMAN &
FLETCHER

THE NIMAN RANCH COOKBOOK

10 TEN SPEED PRESS

FERGUS
HENDERSON

THE WHOLE BEAST

nose to tail eating

ecco

FEARNLEY-
WHITTINGSTALL

MEAT

BOOK

10 TEN SPEED PRESS

PEACE, LOVE, AND BARBECUE

MIKE MILLS AND
AMY MILLS TUNNICLIFFE

MOLLY STEVENS

NORTON

DAVID
TANIS

a platter of figs and other recipes

ARTISAN

ANDREWS

THE
COUNTRY
COOKING
of
IRELAND

CHRONICLE
BOOKS

AND MELISSA CLARK

7 Pro Brisket

"Reading while eating brisket is one of the most voluptuous things that you can do with your time."

—Novelist Gary Shteyngart in an interview with Gigantic magazine

When I first started working on this book, I had no idea how many brisket recipes there were in the world. I figured there were probably just a few basic ones, silly me. As I started my research, I found hundreds in cookbooks. I went online and discovered hundreds more. Maybe thousands. And when I started primary reporting, asking people for truly amazing, totally remarkable brisket recipes, they e-mailed theirs within minutes or texted me or painstakingly wrote out their recipes in longhand. Or had their mother call me from North Carolina.

My conclusion: A lot of brisket recipes are incredibly similar (I'm talking to you, onions and ketchup and wine and brown sugar). A lot are just okay. Some are pretty good. And some—a very few—just reel you in. These are the ones that radiate: "I've got to try this. It sounds amazing/original/so artful/so artless/so simple/authentic/like nothing I've ever made before!" These are a different order of being than

Me: "How do you feel when people say they have the best brisket recipe ever?"

Ari Weinzweig (cofounder, Zingerman's): "I'd never say that. I just want ours to be great. Of course, I come from the kind of family that said, 'What, you only got an A?!'"

the recipes you tear out of the magazine in your doctor's office when no one is looking. What makes them so OMG?

Think imaginative, unlikely ingredients: creamy tahini, palm sugar, spring rhubarb, ripe summer peaches, a splash of aquavit, coarsely crushed coriander seeds, orange zest, black tea. Think magnetic personality: recipes that suggest lovely, clean flavors; unflinching authenticity; dazzling combinations; a deep, dark simmering intensity. Then think descriptions so mouthwatering you can taste them. As the folks at Fatty 'Cue put it: "Our goal is to balance quivering fatty morsels of deliciousness with bright citrus notes, fiery chili heat, rich fermented and briny washes, and complex, unrefined, natural sweetness. Or, in a less obtuse manner, fun, tasty food!"

First we chose the best, then we picked the very very best: recipes boasting astonishing "deliciousness," a marvelous range, and an astounding variety. Here is happiness in melting, molten fork-tender slices.

But lest you think finding these gems was a day at the beach, trust me: we have tested (and discarded) a surprising number of otherwise okay-sounding recipes. Brisket duds. Losers. In the anything goes online world, you never know what to expect. Surprisingly, even recipes from well-known cookbooks and big deal chefs resulted in meat that was bone dry or mushy or stringy. Sauces that were treacly sweet or curdled or overpowering or so hot and smoky that we felt like calling the fire department to put us out.

No . . . don't thank us. It was our job. Our mission. Our pleasure. Hopefully, it is yours, too.

THESE BRISKET RECIPES MADE THE CUT

A Few Housekeeping Notes:

Many brisket recipes are far better made one day ahead and served the next. So be sure you read the recipe through to see if you should begin a day early.

- All of the recipes were tested using kosher salt and freshly ground black pepper unless otherwise specified.

- Don't judge the number of servings by the size of the raw brisket—as mentioned before, the meat shrinks a lot when it cooks. The serving sizes listed are generally based on ½ pound of raw meat per person. The actual number of servings, however, may vary depending on the number of side dishes and people's appetites.

- If you use kosher meat, make sure that you salt sparingly. Add salt to taste.

- Reduce the liquid at the end of cooking if you prefer a richer sauce.

- And, of course, make sure you make enough to have leftovers.

What makes Ardie Davis's brisket so special is that he doesn't add anything special: no mops, no rubs, no foil, no sauce. Yet he turns "plain" into just plain sensational.

BASIC BARBECUE BRISKET

A recipe within a story from Kansas City barbecue expert Ardie Davis

Servings vary

Only the Devil could claim more experience with smoke and heat than Ardie Davis. And Davis has a lot more to show for it. He has worked on several championship barbecue teams; he's written seven barbecue books; he's a judge on the barbecue circuit; he knows everyone who has ever lit a piece of mesquite; he's an esteemed member of the Kansas City Barbeque Society; his longtime smoking and barbecue-eating companion is none other than Paul Kirk, the Baron of Barbecue. And Davis has driven from Memphis to Mobile in search of the tastiest rib and the heartiest rub. Read his books and find out things you never thought possible: from brown sugar brining to getting a good bark on your butt (so to speak). As you can imagine, Davis gets pretty near perfect results with his techniques. Now you can, too.

TAKE IT, ARDIE:

"To barbecue a perfect brisket, you need time and patience. Brisket, a working muscle, is—as you know—naturally tough with lots of connective tissue. Its long, flat shape makes it even more unforgiving to the cook. Look for the biggest, fattest, ugliest brisket you can find. I get the cheapest available unless the fat is yellow, indicating older meat. Untrimmed is important. You need the fat for a tender brisket. Some cooks age the brisket in Cryovac packaging on the bottom shelf of the refrigerator for a week or more, saying it improves the flavor. I don't.

"If I can, I get an 18-pound brisket. From 30 years of looking for meat like that, though, I know you have to go to a restaurant supply place or special-order it from a butcher or get lucky and find one at a wholesale club like BJ's. Whatever size brisket you use, you're going to lose at least 40 percent during the cooking process, so figure on 6 to 8 ounces of raw meat per person. A 10-pound raw brisket, which will serve about 12 hungry guests, will take at least 15 hours at a grill temperature of about 225°F. The rule of thumb is 1½ to 2 hours per pound. Patience with the process, waiting until the right moment to take the brisket out of the cooker, will be rewarded.

"After removing the meat from the packaging, trim the fat to about ¼-inch thickness. When it comes to seasoning the meat, I prefer a simple light dusting of pepper and salt, either overnight or right before the brisket goes in the grill; this really lets the flavor of the meat shine through. Some people also like to use some kind of fat, like butter or olive oil, and/or sugar, which is fine. Using a more complex rub and/or baste is optional. I suggest that you try the basic way before experimenting with rubs or bastes because it is important to know how 'plain' barbecue brisket tastes. Then you'll be able to judge for yourself whether or not a rub or baste enhances the flavor.

"For barbecuing the brisket, I like to use a 22½-inch Weber kettle grill, which is versatile enough for large briskets, turkey, pork butt, and anything shy of a piglet or whole hog. No modifications are needed to barbecue in a standard grill or smoker as opposed to commercial equipment. For the fire, I use Kingsford charcoal briquettes. Have 18 pounds at hand, although you likely won't need it all, and light them in a chimney starter. Putting 3 to 4 cups of water-soaked wood chips on top of the briquettes creates the smoke that flavors the meat. I usually use pecan and apple chips; other options are hickory, oak, cherry, alder, mesquite, or sweet maple. Just be sure to first soak the chips in water for at least 40 minutes, preferably overnight. (Chips work best in a kettle grill; wood chunks or small logs, which don't need to be soaked, work best in a large grill with an offset firebox. Whatever type and form of wood you choose, don't use trimmings from a lumberyard unless you're positive the wood hasn't been treated with chemicals.)

"After you've soaked your chips, lit your charcoal in the chimney starter, and trimmed and seasoned your brisket, remove the cooking grate from the grill and set it aside (if it isn't already clean, clean it with a wire brush before removing it). To monitor the temperature inside the grill, stick the bulb end of a candy thermometer in the top lid vent. Wrap enough Scotch tape around the bottom of the thermometer to prevent it from falling into the grill. When the charcoal is gray, dump it on the coal grate to one side of the grill and close the lid. (If you're not using a chimney starter, start the briquettes directly on the coal grate on one side of the grill.)

"When the temperature inside the grill reaches 225°F to 250°F, dump the drained wood chips directly over the coals. (The higher end of the temperature range is advisable for the first 30 to 45 minutes or so of cooking; it gives the meat "bark.") Return the cooking grate to the grill, spray the grate area opposite the coals with cooking oil, then place the brisket, fat side up, opposite the coals. (You don't want to grill a brisket. It will be tough as a shoe. You need to cook it with indirect heat.) Lid the grill immediately.

"Regularly monitor the temperature while the brisket cooks. Control air to the coals using the bottom vents; more air will increase the temperature inside the grill. My Weber will go a minimum of 4 hours before needing more hot coals. More often than not, new coals won't be needed for 6 to 8 hours. However, each grill—even the same brand and model—is different, so get to know your grill. When I see that the grill temperature is getting low, I sometimes add new briquettes atop the old ones when the old ones are still alive enough to ignite the new coals. Most times, though, I fire up at least half a chimney starterful and add them when they're gray and hot to the almost-spent old briquettes. (Do not add new wood chips when you add new coals; excessive smoke will impart a bitterness to the meat.)

"Some cooks wrap the brisket in aluminum foil (The Texas Crutch) after 6 to 8 hours and cook it that way for the duration. Others say this method yields 'pot roast.' The debate is never-ending. I used to use foil, but am now weaned from it. If you do opt for foil, before you seal up the meat, try coating it with a little honey and a non-salty beef stock for added flavor and moisture.

"Although I can tell when the brisket is done by how tender it is when I touch it, unless you're experienced at this, I suggest using a good instant-read meat thermometer. Check the brisket occasionally, starting about an hour or so before its estimated done time, by sticking the thermometer horizontally into the thickest part of the meat; when the temperature reads between 180 and 200°F, it's ready. (For slices, go for the lower temperature; it's fall-apart tender at 200°F.) If you want to learn how to determine doneness by using the touch method, prod the finished brisket with your forefinger a few times in different areas. Remember how the meat feels and test yourself the next time you barbecue brisket by using both the touch method and an instant-read thermometer. With practice, you'll know exactly what a properly cooked brisket feels like. Remove the brisket to a cutting board with a meat fork, cover loosely with foil, and allow it to rest for 40 to 50 minutes. Trim any excess fat before slicing the meat, and be sure to cut the meat against the grain. Texans like thick slices. Kansas Citians like it thinner. Take a bite. If your brisket is tender (not mushy) and flavorful, congratulations. You have mastered one of the most difficult cuts of meat to barbecue."

LOVE THAT ARDIE!!!

Baked beans with burnt ends, bread, dill pickle slices, and hot and mild sauce from Johnny's BBQ, Mission, Kansas. Does it get any better?

TENDER SLOW-COOKED BEEF BRISKET

Adapted from My Family Table: A Passionate Plea For Home Cooking by John Besh, Andrews McMeel, 2011

Serves 10

John Besh is one of the most well-known and lauded chefs in America. Awards like best chef, best cuisine, best restaurant keep on coming. He now runs seven good-luck-getting-a-reservation restaurants: his flagship, August, Lüke in New Orleans, an offshoot Lüke in San Antonio, La Provence, Domenica, Besh Steak, and The American Sector. His first book, My New Orleans, continues to be a best-seller. While Besh is a superstar chef, he is also a husband and father: thus this uncomplicated, crowd-pleasing recipe that he has created for home cooks.

Chef Besh believes that smoking a brisket, when done properly, is an art, especially in the South. With this recipe, Besh makes art lovers out of all of us. The night before, he generously seasons the brisket with the dry rub on all sides, then wraps well in plastic wrap and refrigerates it overnight. The next day he lets the brisket pick up its wonderful smoky flavor outside, then wraps it well and finishes it indoors in a low oven so it's falling-apart tender.

BRISKET

1   (5- to 6-pound) beef brisket

½   cup Dry Rub (recipe follows)

Preheat the smoker to 250°F. Lay the brisket in the smoker and smoke for 6 hours, adding wood as needed along the way to maintain a near-perfect 250°F temperature. It's important to remember to adjust the dampers to regulate the heat. When the brisket is tender, remove it from the smoker, wrap it in aluminum foil, and place in a 200°F oven for an additional 2 hours to continue the slow cooking process toward perfection.

To serve, trim away the excess fat (Besh likes to add it to homemade baked beans; it improves the flavor), and slice against the grain.

DRY RUB

Makes about 3½ cups

Besh says, "This rub is quite classic but it works well, too, as a brine for meat and poultry when diluted with enough water to cover—so you've got the perfect combination of salty/sweet. Or, use the dry base as a wet rub, adding just enough olive oil to form a paste. It's wonderful slathered on a whole leg of lamb."

1	cup brown sugar
1	cup Kosher salt
1	tablespoon freshly ground black pepper
1	tablespoon pimentón
1	tablespoon garlic powder
1	tablespoon onion powder
¼	teaspoon cayenne pepper

In a small bowl, mix the ingredients together and store in a Mason jar. Tightly sealed, it will keep for about 2 weeks in the refrigerator.

When ready to use, rub the meat well, preferably the night before you cook it. (Just store the rubbed meat well wrapped in plastic in the refrigerator overnight.)

John Besh with his wife, Jenifer; his mother, Imelda; and two of his four sons. See photo of his brisket on p. 83.

BRANDING BRISKET WITH BO'S BARBECUE SAUCE

Adapted from the The Niman Ranch Cookbook, by Bill Niman and Janet Fletcher, Ten Speed Press, 2005

Serves 10–12

No one knows beef (or pork or lamb!) better than the folks at Niman. Their oven-braised brisket gets its jolt from a sensational barbecue sauce. The recipe comes from two members of the Niman's extended ranch family—Bo McSwine, owner of Bo's BBQ in California, gets credit for the rich and tangy sauce. Oregon cattle rancher Debbie Bentz contributed the brisket portion of this recipe. She recommends that you use the point, not the flat.

BRISKET

	Kosher salt and freshly ground black pepper
2	tablespoons olive oil
1	(6-pound) beef brisket
2	yellow onions, thinly sliced
10	sprigs thyme
1	cup dry red wine
2	cups beef stock

SAUCE

1	tablespoon olive oil
½	small yellow onion, minced
1	clove garlic, minced
1	cup ketchup
3	tablespoons freshly squeezed lemon juice
2	tablespoons Worcestershire sauce
3	tablespoons brown sugar
1	teaspoon dry mustard
½	teaspoon freshly ground black pepper
¼	teaspoon crushed red pepper
	Kosher salt

Preheat the oven to 350°F.

To prepare the brisket, pat it dry with a paper towel and season with salt and pepper to taste. Heat 1 tablespoon of the oil in a large, high-sided ovenproof sauté pan with a lid over high heat. Add the brisket and cook, turning once, for 2 to 3 minutes per side, until lightly browned. Transfer to a plate.

Add the remaining tablespoon of olive oil to the pan and reduce the heat to medium-high. Add the onions and thyme and cook, stirring often, for about 3 minutes, or until the onions begin to brown. Add the wine and cook for 1 minute. Add the stock, bring to a boil, return the brisket to the pan, cover, and bake until fork-tender, 3 to 4 hours.

Remove the brisket from the oven, transfer to a plate, and let cool to room temperature. Cover with plastic wrap and refrigerate for at least 4 hours, or until chilled enough to slice easily. Discard the pan juices.

The grass is always greener . . .

To prepare the sauce, heat the olive oil in a small saucepan over medium-high heat. Add the onion and garlic and cook, stirring often, for 2 to 3 minutes, until soft. Stir in the ketchup, lemon juice, Worcestershire sauce, brown sugar, mustard, black pepper, and crushed red pepper. Bring to a boil and cook for 2 to 3 minutes, until the sugar melts. Season to taste with salt, then taste and adjust the seasonings. Let cool, cover, and refrigerate until needed.

BARBECUE GREEN CHiLE BRiSKET

Adapted from a recipe by Chef Josh Baum, Josh's Barbecue, Santa Fe, New Mexico

Serves 6–8

Baum uses fresh New Mexican green chiles when they are in season. Otherwise, he uses frozen ones, which aren't readily available outside the area. You can mail-order them from buenofoods.com. There is a minimum, though, and the shipping is costly. Good news: Anaheim chiles can be substituted.

1	(4-pound) beef brisket
1	quart chopped green chiles, fresh or frozen (see Note)
	Kosher salt and coarsely ground black pepper
1½	tablespoons granulated garlic
2	tablespoons corn oil
2	cups chicken or beef stock, if needed
½	large yellow onion, finely diced
1	tablespoon cornstarch

Preheat a smoker or grill to 220°F, using charcoal briquettes with soaked and drained wood chips on top or all wood (not mesquite) set off to one side of the vessel.

Season the brisket evenly with equal parts salt and pepper. Place it in the smoker or grill on the side opposite the heat source, shut the lid, and cook until the meat reaches 160°F on an instant-read thermometer, about 5 hours. While it's cooking, maintain the grill temperature at about 220°F, adding more briquettes or wood as necessary.

Remove the brisket and tightly double-wrap it in heavy-duty aluminum foil. Place the brisket back into the smoker or grill and continue to cook at 220°F until the meat reaches 200°F on an instant-read thermometer, about 4 hours. (Note: The second round of cooking can be done in an oven set to 220°F, but you won't get the same smoky flavor.)

Remove the brisket and carefully transfer the meat from the foil to a cutting board, saving the juices in the foil in the process. Strain the juices into a medium pot and bring to a boil, skimming away the excess fat. Set the juices aside. Trim the fat from the brisket and chop the meat into roughly ¾-inch cubes, then set aside.

In a large heavy-bottomed pot, heat the oil over medium heat, then add the onion and sauté until translucent, 6 to 8 minutes. Add the brisket, chiles, granulated garlic, and 2 cups of the reserved brisket juices. (If you don't have 2 cups of juices, make up the difference with chicken or beef stock.) Cook at a low simmer for 20 minutes. Combine the cornstarch with 3 tablespoons water, then stir into the brisket mixture. Cook for an additional 10 minutes on low heat, stirring occasionally. Season with salt and pepper.

NOTE: If using fresh chiles, which is preferable, they must first be roasted, peeled, and seeded; start with about 3½ pounds.

CLASSIC BRAISED BEEF BRISKET

From Chef Todd Gray, Equinox Restaurant, Washington, D.C.

Serves 6

Todd Gray, who is as modest as
his restaurant is famous.

2 tablespoons salt

1 tablespoon smoked paprika

1 tablespoon mustard seed

1 teaspoon freshly ground black
pepper

1 (3-pound) beef brisket, trimmed

2 tablespoons vegetable oil

2 sprigs rosemary

2 sprigs thyme

3 cloves garlic, crushed

1 quart veal stock

1 cup dry red wine

½ cup balsamic vinegar

*Think of Chef Gray as the Mozart of Virginia Angus beef,
perfectly orchestrating every note and harmonizing all
the flavors in a brisket that sings with fresh flavor, seduces
with heady aromas, dazzles with a drizzle of shiny sauce.
You will ask for an encore. On a Mozartian housekeeping
note, you can substitute beef stock for veal stock.*

In a small bowl, combine the salt, paprika, mustard seed,
and pepper. Rub the brisket all over with the spice mix. In
a large heavy skillet, heat the oil over medium-high heat
until hot. Add the brisket and brown evenly on both sides, 5
to 7 minutes per side. Transfer the brisket to an ovenproof
baking dish just large enough to hold the brisket snugly,
then add the rosemary and thyme sprigs, garlic, stock, wine,
and vinegar. Cover the dish with heavy-duty aluminum foil
and bake until the brisket is fork-tender, 3 to 4 hours.

Transfer the brisket to a cutting board and cover with foil
to keep warm. Strain the liquid into a pan and reduce
over medium heat to about 2½ cups. The finished
sauce should have a glaze-like consistency. Check the
seasonings. Slice the brisket against the grain and serve
drizzled with the sauce.

NOTE: With a slight adjustment, this brisket also stars in
Gray's restaurant, with a few tweaks to make it a touch more
refined. The chef says that at Equinox he weights down the
cooked and cooled meat in the fridge for about an hour.
This helps to compress it, tightening the texture. Slice the
meat after it has been compressed. Next, gently reheat on
the stove in the cooking liquid before you reduce it.

BRAISED FRESH BRISKET IN STOUT WITH ONIONS

Adapted from Simon Hopkinson's Second Helpings of Roast Chicken, Hyperion, 2001

Serves 4

The saucy British chef and writer Simon Hopkinson believes that what the world needs today is simple, old-fashioned food made from the finest ingredients, hence this gloriously rich, deeply delicious stew. If you can't find mushroom ketchup, Hopkinson suggests substituting Worcestershire sauce, using a little less because it is spicier.

1   **(2-pound) beef brisket**

    Salt and freshly ground black pepper

3   **tablespoons all-purpose flour**

2   **tablespoons beef dripping or lard**

8   **tablespoons (1 stick) butter**

3⅓ **pounds onions, peeled and sliced**

3 to 4 **tablespoons red wine vinegar**

1   **tablespoon mushroom ketchup**

1   **tablespoon anchovy paste**

1   **cup stout**

1   **cup beef stock**

2   **bay leaves**

2   **tablespoons chopped fresh parsley leaves**

Preheat the oven to 275°F. Season the brisket all over with salt and pepper, then dredge with flour. Melt the dripping or lard in a deep cast-iron lidded casserole dish until very hot. Sear the meat on all surfaces and remove to a plate. Pour off all of the fat, then add the butter; there is a lot of it, but this is necessary to cope with the large amount of onions. Allow the butter to become fully melted and turn frothy and toasty-smelling before carefully tipping in the onions. Stir them around thoroughly in the butter until well coated and do not add any salt (this can prevent the onions from browning). Gently sweat over very low heat with the lid on, stirring from time to time, until they have flopped down into the bottom of the pan as a slippery muddle; this can take anything up to 30 to 40 minutes or so.

Turn the heat up a little now and, stirring more frequently, allow the onions to color to a deep, rich, golden brown. Add the vinegar, allow it to bubble furiously, and drive most of it off over full heat until the onions are dry and buttery once more. Stir in the mushroom ketchup, anchovy paste, stout, stock, and bay leaves. Bring up to a simmer and remove any scum that forms on the surface with a ladle. Slip the beef back into the pot and bury it under the onions and liquid. Cover with a sheet of wax paper cut to fit the dimensions of the pot and press gently down upon the surface. Put on the lid and cook in the oven for 1½ to 2 hours, or until completely tender when poked with a skewer. Check for seasoning and stir in some of the parsley. Remove the beef to a cutting board, trim the fat, and slice against the grain. Serve the meat and the contents of the pot in deep soup plates and sprinkle with the rest of the parsley.

BRİSKET İN SWEET-AND-SOUR SAUCE

Adapted from Levana's Table by Levana Kirschenbaum (Stewart, Tabori & Chang, 2002)

Serves 12–14

Kirschenbaum's modern spin on sweet-and-sour brisket is wonderfully simple: the sauce is quickly made in a food processor. Her delicious Asian-inspired recipe is redolent with cloves, ginger, honey, and soy sauce. The All-American twist is the bubbly sweet fizz that comes from Coca-Cola. ("Never mind the weird ingredients. They work!" enthuses Kirschenbaum.) If the meat browns too quickly during the second baking period, cover the top loosely with aluminum foil. If the pan seems dry, add a little water.

SAUCE

1	medium onion, quartered
	One 2-inch piece fresh ginger, peeled
6	large cloves garlic, peeled
¼	cup Dijon mustard
½	cup dry red wine
½	cup Coca-Cola or ginger ale
1	cup ketchup
¼	cup honey
¼	cup cider vinegar
¼	cup soy sauce
½	cup olive oil
½	teaspoon ground cloves
1	teaspoon each sea salt and coarsely ground black pepper
1	(6- to 7-pound) first-cut beef brisket, rinsed and patted thoroughly dry

Preheat the oven to 350°F.

For the sauce, process all the sauce ingredients in a food processor until smooth. Place the brisket in a pan just big enough to fit it and pour on the marinade.

Cover tightly with a double layer of aluminum foil and bake for 2 hours. Turn the brisket over and bake uncovered for 1 more hour. Transfer the brisket to a cutting board.

Transfer the sauce to a saucepan and reduce to about 2½ cups. Skim the oil off the top.

Let the brisket cool slightly. Slice thin against the grain (if the slices look too long, cut the brisket in half across its whole length before slicing). Pour the gravy on top and serve hot.

BRISKET WITH GINGER, ORANGE PEEL AND TOMATO

Adapted from Joan Nathan's Quiches, Kugels, and Couscous, Knopf, 2010

Serves 6–10

Daniel Rose is a young American chef with his own restaurant (Spring) in Paris. (One recent cyber rave: "Spring in the 1st: Pow, Wow, Zap, Izt!") Here, Rose has used his considerable superpowers to create a contemporary classic, at once refined and robust. The lemon and orange—literally and figuratively—give it equal amounts of American zest and French style.

1	(3- to 5-pound) beef brisket, trimmed
	Salt and freshly ground black pepper
2	tablespoons vegetable oil
12	small spring onions, trimmed and halved, or 2 medium onions, peeled and thickly sliced
6	carrots, peeled
8	cloves garlic, peeled
1	tablespoon cider vinegar
1	cup dry white wine
3	cups veal, beef, or chicken stock
3	small tomatoes, halved
2	sprigs fresh thyme, or ½ teaspoon dried thyme
1	bay leaf
5	sprigs fresh parsley, plus ¼ cup chopped
1	(½-inch) slice fresh ginger
	Green top of 1 leek
2	lemons
2	oranges

Preheat the oven to 325°F.

Season the brisket with salt and pepper to taste. Pour the oil into a Dutch oven over medium heat. Brown the meat for about 4 minutes on each side. Remove and set aside. Add the onions, carrots, and garlic to the Dutch oven, cooking until they are just beginning to soften, adding more oil if necessary. Raise the heat, pour in the vinegar, and stir with a wooden spoon to scrape up any bits that have stuck to the pan. Add the white wine and continue stirring, allowing the liquid to reduce for a few minutes.

Put the meat back in the pot, along with the stock. Bring to a simmer, and add the tomatoes, thyme, bay leaf, parsley sprigs, ginger, and leek top.

Using a straight peeler, remove the zest in long strips from one of the lemons and one of the oranges. Add to the pot. Cover and place in the oven for 45 minutes.

Lower the oven temperature to 275°F, and continue cooking for 2 to 2½ hours more, or until fork-tender.

Remove the meat and vegetables from the pot. Discard the citrus peels, thyme, parsley sprigs, ginger, bay leaf, and leek top. If cooking in advance, let the pot cool and refrigerate the brisket in the sauce.

Before serving, remove the meat from the sauce and slice on the bias against the grain. Put the meat back in the sauce, and reheat in a warm oven or on the stovetop. Arrange the meat on a serving platter along with the vegetables.

Strain the sauce into a pan, then reduce it over high heat to concentrate the flavor and thicken it. Pour the sauce over the sliced brisket, and, before serving, sprinkle with the grated zests of the remaining lemon and orange and the chopped parsley.

Daniel Rose, right, oversees a dish at his restaurant, Spring, in Paris.

His name in lights! Cowboy/cook Tom Perini at the Perini Ranch.

TEXAS OVEN-ROASTED BEEF BRİSKET

Adapted from a recipe by Tom Perini, Perini Ranch, Buffalo Gap, Texas

Serves 8

With a lightly spiced browned crust and mega Texas-size smokehouse flavor, cowboy/cook Tom Perini comes up with a knockout recipe that lets you oven roast your way to brisket bliss. Just rub, roast, braise—done. Paula Deen loves Perini's cooking, too: check out The Food Network to see a video of Perini showing Paula his skills.

2	tablespoons chili powder
2	tablespoons salt
1	tablespoon garlic powder
1	tablespoon onion powder
1	tablespoon ground black pepper
1	tablespoon sugar
2	teaspoons dry mustard
1	bay leaf, crushed
1	(4-pound) beef brisket, trimmed
1½	cups beef stock

Preheat the oven to 350°F.

In a small bowl, make a dry rub by combining the chili powder, salt, garlic and onion powders, pepper, sugar, dry mustard, and bay leaf. Season the brisket all over with the rub. Place the brisket in a roasting pan and roast in the oven, uncovered, for 1 hour.

Add the beef stock and enough water to yield about ½ inch of liquid in the roasting pan, then tightly cover the pan with aluminum foil. Lower the oven temperature to 300°F and continue cooking until the brisket is fork-tender, about 3 hours.

Transfer the brisket to a cutting board, trim any excess fat, and thinly slice the meat against the grain. Serve with the pan juices.

BEEF BRİSKET WİTH TANGY PEACHES

From Chef/Owner John Shields, Gertrude's, The Baltimore Museum of Art

Serves 8

Inspired by southern Maryland braised ribs, this is one of the few summer briskets. The sweetness of fresh ripe peaches is tempered by tart apple cider vinegar, deepened by cinnamon and cloves. When this beauty is ready to eat, you don't know whether to dig in or call the paparazzi. If you can't wait until peach season, Chef Shields suggests individually frozen peaches (available on Amazon). Shields sometimes uses fresh apricots instead of peaches.

3	tablespoons rendered beef fat or vegetable oil
1	(4-pound) beef brisket, trimmed
2	onions, peeled and chopped
2	carrots, peeled and chopped
3	cloves garlic, peeled
3	cups beef stock
¼	cup brown sugar ¼ cup apple cider vinegar
6	cups peeled, sliced semi-firm fresh peaches
2	bay leaves
1	scant teaspoon ground cinnamon
½	teaspoon ground cloves
	Salt and freshly ground black pepper

In an ovenproof enameled cast-iron pot or other heavy pot with a tight-fitting lid just large enough to hold the brisket snugly, heat the oil over medium-high heat until hot. Add the brisket and brown well on both sides, 5 to 7 minutes per side. Transfer the brisket to a large platter and set aside. Reduce the heat to medium, add the onions, carrots, and garlic to the pot, and sauté, stirring occasionally, for about 10 minutes.

Return the brisket to the pot and add the beef stock. Bring the stock to a boil, scraping the bottom of the pot to release any browned bits, and add the brown sugar, vinegar, and 4 cups of the sliced peaches. Stir in the bay leaves, cinnamon, and cloves. Season with salt and pepper. Bring the liquid back to a boil, then reduce the heat to a simmer, cover the pot, and cook the brisket until fork-tender, 2½ to 3 hours. Turn the brisket over several times during the cooking process.

When the brisket is done, transfer the meat to a cutting board and cover with aluminum foil to keep warm. Push the braising liquid through a coarse strainer into a pot. Skim off any fat, then bring the liquid to a boil and reduce it by about one-third. The sauce should be full-flavored and slightly syrupy; if it's not, reduce it a little further. Add the remaining sliced peaches and warm gently. Adjust the seasonings. Slice the brisket against the grain and place on a warm platter. Serve with the peach gravy on the side.

BARBECUED BRISKET SANDWICHES
(WITH FIRECRACKER SAUCE)

Adapted from a recipe by Chef David Page, Shinn Estate Vineyards and former owner of Home

Serves 8

Thinly sliced and slathered with barbecue sauce, this is the perfect summer brisket. And the meat tastes terrific even before smoking, so if you don't have a grill handy, you can still enjoy it.

2   tablespoons coarsely ground coriander

2   tablespoons coarsely ground cumin

2   tablespoons coarsely ground yellow mustard seed

2   tablespoons hot paprika

1   tablespoon ancho chile powder

1   tablespoon freshly ground black pepper

1   tablespoon kosher salt

1   teaspoon dried ginger

1   (5-pound) beef brisket, trimmed

½   cup hardwood chips (optional), soaked in 1 cup water for 30 minutes

3   tablespoons olive oil

2   cups diced yellow onions

2   tablespoons minced garlic

2   tablespoons apple cider vinegar

2   tablespoons dark brown sugar

2   tablespoons Worcestershire sauce

2   tablespoons soy sauce

4   cups peeled, seeded, and chopped tomatoes; or 1(28-ounce) can diced tomatoes and their juices

8   potato rolls

Preheat the oven to 300°F. For the rub, in a small bowl, combine the first eight ingredients. Place the brisket on a work surface and pat the rub over the entire surface of the brisket, rubbing the spices into the meat until it is coated. (If some of the spices don't adhere to the meat, add them to the braising pan with the meat later.)

For cooking and serving the brisket, heat the oil over medium heat in a braising pan large enough to fit the brisket. Add the onions and garlic and gently cook until softened, 5 to 10 minutes. Add the vinegar, brown sugar, Worcestershire sauce, and soy sauce and simmer briefly. Add the tomatoes, then place the brisket on top. Cover the pan with a tight-fitting lid or with heavy-duty aluminum foil and place in the oven. Cook until fork-tender, about 4 hours, turning the brisket over twice.

Prepare a charcoal grill. Let the fire burn down and knock down the coals so that you have a low fire. If using, drain the wood chips and add to the fire. Remove the brisket from the pan and reserve the sauce. Place the brisket on the grill and close the lid. Damper the grill and cook over the lowest heat possible and with as much smoke as possible for 45 minutes to 1 hour.

Defat the reserved sauce, transfer to a saucepan, place over medium heat, and simmer to thicken, about 10 minutes. Transfer the sauce to a blender or food processor and purée until smooth. Season to taste with salt and pepper. Thinly slice against the grain; serve on potato rolls with the sauce.

SEPHARDIC BRISKET

Adapted from Chef Jim Cohen, Chef/Partner, The Empire Restaurant, Louisville, Colorado

Serves 8

This showstopper was created by Jim Cohen, who has both updated and upended tradition. Black tea? Pasilla chiles? Sweet fruit? Use ancho chiles if you can't find pasillas.

2	dried pasilla chiles
1	(4-pound) beef brisket, trimmed
	Salt and freshly ground black pepper
	All-purpose flour, for dredging
¼	cup olive oil
2	onions, diced
2	tablespoons peeled and chopped fresh ginger
1	cup freshly squeezed orange juice
4	cups chicken or beef stock or water, more if necessary
1	cinnamon stick
1	bay leaf
1	teaspoon peppercorns
4	tea bags strong black tea
2	cups dried pitted prunes
2	cups dried apricots

Preheat the oven to 400°F. Soak the chiles in lukewarm water for 30 minutes. Seed them, remove the stems, chop the flesh into tiny pieces, and set aside.

Season the brisket with salt and pepper to taste and dredge with flour. Heat the oil in a heavy roasting pan just large enough to hold the brisket snugly and brown the brisket on both sides, 5 to 7 minutes per side. Remove from the pan.

In the same pan, over medium heat, add the onions and ginger and sauté, stirring occasionally, until the onions are transparent. Add the reserved chiles and deglaze with the orange juice. Reduce the liquid by half. Add the brisket and enough stock or water to cover the meat. Add the cinnamon stick, bay leaf, and peppercorns. Place in the oven and cook, uncovered, until the brisket is tender, about 3 hours, turning at 30-minute intervals.

Transfer the brisket to a platter. Remove the cinnamon stick and bay leaf from the liquid and pour it into a food processor or blender. Purée until smooth. If the sauce is too thin or not flavorful enough, reduce in a pan over medium heat. Cool the meat and the sauce separately, then cover and refrigerate for a few hours or overnight.

When ready to serve, preheat the oven to 350°F. Bring 4 cups of water to a boil. In a large bowl, steep the tea bags in the water to make a strong tea. Discard the bags. Put the prunes and apricots in the tea to plump for about 30 minutes, then drain them. Meanwhile, slice the brisket against the grain and place the slices in a pan. Remove the congealed fat and pour the sauce over the brisket. Add the fruit to the sauce, cover the pan with aluminum foil, and heat the brisket in the oven until hot, about 45 minutes. Check the seasonings before serving.

BRİSKET İN TAHİNA SAUCE

An Israeli-American dish, adapted from Joan Nathan's Jewish Cooking in America, Knopf, 1994

Serves 8–10

If you love tahina (the other name of tahini, when pronounced in Hebrew), the lush sesame seed paste, this is the brisket for you. It's very rich and a little goes a long way. Nathan credits Israeli-born home cook Dalia Carmel for this recipe. After eating a brisket cooked in coconut milk in a Malay restaurant in New York, Carmel conjured up a Middle Eastern–style brisket. The tahina in this lovely hybrid adds a creamy richness; the pineapple juice tenderizes the meat.

1	envelope onion soup mix
1	cup canned pineapple juice
1	large onion, finely sliced
1	cup beef broth, plus extra if needed
1	cup tahina
2	cloves garlic, mashed
	Salt and freshly ground black pepper, plus extra if needed
½	cup freshly squeezed lemon juice
1	(4-pound) beef brisket, trimmed

Preheat the oven to 350°F.

In a large bowl, combine the onion soup mix, pineapple juice, broth, tahina, garlic, salt and pepper to taste, lemon juice, and ¼ cup water.

Trim the brisket of most of the fat. Place in a shallow baking pan and rub with the onion-tahina mixture, making sure there is at least 2 inches of liquid beneath the meat. If there's not enough, add more water. Scatter the sliced onion on top.

Bake, covered with heavy-duty aluminum foil, for 2 to 3 hours, or until the meat is fork-tender. If it is too dry after an hour, add more broth or pineapple juice.

When done, remove the meat from the sauce and cool. Refrigerate the sauce so that the fat can be removed. Slice the meat against the grain and place it in a pan. Cover with the sauce. If it is too thick, again blend in some pineapple juice or water to thin it out. When ready to serve, preheat the oven to 350°F. Cover and heat in the oven until hot, about 45 minutes, and serve.

AQUAVİT BRİSKET

From Andreas Viestad, Norwegian food columnist and television chef; host of New Scandinavian Cooking

Serves 8–10

This luscious brisket is really a soup—it embraces the bold ingredients and bracing spirit of today's Scandinavian cuisine. Chef Viestad adds five different herbs and spices to the meat. Then he finishes the shimmering broth with aquavit, the Scandinavian liquor that often has caraway as the predominant spice. If you can't find aquavit, substitute gin or omit the alcohol altogether—the recipe is still great without it. As with most brisket dishes, this dish is even better the next day; gently reheat on the stove.

4	teaspoons caraway seed
4	teaspoons coriander seed, coarsely crushed
2	teaspoons cumin seed
2	teaspoons dill seed
2	teaspoons fennel seed
1	(4-pound) beef brisket, trimmed and cut into 1½-inch cubes
3	tablespoons butter
3	large onions, chopped
9	cloves garlic, chopped
8	celery ribs, cut into 1-inch pieces
6	carrots, peeled and chopped
⅓	cup Aquavit

Preheat the oven to 350°F.

In a large bowl, combine all of the spices. Add the brisket and mix well. Heat a large heavy pot over medium-high heat. Working in batches, if necessary, add the brisket and sear in the dry pot, stirring frequently until the spices are slightly charred and the meat is browned on all sides.

Remove the brisket and set aside, then reduce the heat to medium-low. Add the butter and allow it to melt. Add the onions and garlic and cook, stirring occasionally, until the onions are soft and slightly caramelized, about 15 minutes. Add the celery and carrots and cook, stirring occasionally, for about 5 minutes. Add the brisket and continue cooking, stirring occasionally, for 10 minutes. Add 1 quart of water and stir to combine. The water should just cover the ingredients; if it doesn't, add more.

Bring the liquid to a boil, then reduce the heat, cover the pot, and simmer until the meat is tender, 3 to 4 hours. Remove the cover for the last 20 minutes or so of cooking. Just before serving, add the aquavit. Allow the broth to simmer for 5 minutes. Check the seasonings, then serve in soup bowls.

BRISKET NOODLE SOUP WITH KOREAN CHILE

From Chef Anita Lo, restaurant annisa, New York

Serves 4

Could we be any luckier than to get chef Anita Lo to create a brisket recipe just for this book? Spicy, soulful, artfully balanced—at once exotic and familiar—this sublime soup is comfort food for the gods. And goddesses. Look for the Asian ingredients at Asian grocers, the international aisle at your supermarket, or online. Dried anchovies come in a variety of sizes—you want the ones that are about 2 inches long. The quality of fish sauce varies greatly: Squid and Three Crabs are two reputable brands. If you like lots of noodles (who doesn't?), feel free to add an extra pack.

SOUP

1   tablespoon toasted sesame oil

1   tablespoon vegetable or canola oil

1   small onion, cut into about ¼-inch slices

3   cloves garlic, chopped

2   tablespoons Korean ground red chile (gochu garu)

1   sheet dashi kombu, rinsed

8   dried anchovies (iriko)

3   scallions, white parts only, halved lengthwise

2   quarts water

1   cup peeled, quartered, and sliced (about ⅓-inch thick) daikon radish

1   cup halved and sliced (about ⅓-inch thick) zucchini

2   tablespoons soy sauce

3   tablespoons fish sauce

    Granulated sugar, to taste

MARINADE

1   tablespoon granulated sugar

2   tablespoons soy sauce

1   clove garlic, chopped

    Salt

    Freshly ground black pepper

1¼ pounds beef brisket, preferably second cut, trimmed

NOODLES

3   (7-ounce) packages refrigerated or frozen udon noodles

1   tablespoon thinly sliced scallions, green parts only (sliced on the bias)

What Anita Lo Brings to Brisket

Anita Lo, outside her restaurant, ready for kitchen combat with her Misono slicer.

American chef Anita Lo's heritage is Chinese. Her background, multicultural. Her culinary training, classically French. After graduating first in her class at the Ritz-Escoffier—with honors—she has gone on to earn just about every accolade and award for her highly original cuisine.

Iron Chef America: Season One, Chef Lo vs. Mario Batali. Sorry, Mario.

New York Magazine's Adam Platt calls a meal at her New York restaurant, annisa, "an experience that strikes that delicate (and increasingly rare) balance between modern style, classic technique, and pure, old-fashioned gourmet pleasure."

Having taken on Mario Batali, she now takes on brisket. Lucky for us, she has been eating—and loving—it since she was a child . . .

. . ."We had corned beef and cabbage on occasion—the fatty part is best—and I had a pastrami sandwich every day packed into my school lunch for perhaps years," she says. "One of my nannies made pot roast on occasion, and I don't remember what cut of meat it was, but it could have been brisket."

Chef Lo adds, "I don't remember any Asian preparations at home, but we did go out for Korean food on occasion and that cut plays a prominent role in Korean cuisine; also in pho bo, which we also had on occasion when we went out for Vietnamese food. There's also a Shanghai dish (my dad was from Shanghai) that I think I had when I was growing up—I don't remember what it's called—but I think it sandwiches braised brisket in between two sesame flatbreads."

This is how new brisket memories are made.

Preheat the oven to 350°F.

For the marinade, in a medium bowl, combine the sugar, soy sauce, garlic, and salt and pepper to taste. Cut the brisket into two or more pieces against the grain, so that the pieces are about 2 inches wide. Add to the bowl and coat with the marinade. Set aside.

For the soup, in a large pot over medium heat, add the oils and heat until hot. Add the onion and cook, stirring until translucent, about 3 minutes. Add the garlic and ground chile and stir briefly. Add the marinated brisket (and any excess marinade) and stir, then add the kombu, anchovies, scallion whites, and water. Raise the heat to high, bring the liquid to a boil and skim, then reduce the heat so that the liquid simmers gently. Keep the meat submerged by placing a heatproof plate over it or burying it under the kombu, and cook until fork tender, about 3½ hours. Occasionally stir the liquid and replenish water as needed. You want to end up with slightly less liquid than you started with.

Remove the meat, shred it into bite-size pieces, removing excess fat if necessary, and set aside. Remove the kombu, cut it into bite-size strips, and return to the pot. Bring the liquid to the boil, skim off any fat, then add the daikon and boil until it starts to lose its crispness, 3 to 4 minutes. Add the zucchini and boil until crisp tender, 2 to 3 minutes. Turn off the heat, stir in the fish sauce and soy sauce, then taste the soup. Add the sugar (start with about 1 teaspoon) and salt and pepper to taste. The soup should have a really "round" flavor and great depth. You do not want to taste the sugar or any sweetness.

For the noodles, in a medium pot, heat the noodles according to the package instructions. (Salt the water, though, and do not use the accompanying packets of soup base.) Divide the noodles among four soup bowls. Top with the shredded brisket, then pour over the soup and vegetables. (Discard the anchovies if you like.) Garnish with the scallion greens and serve immediately.

"If Chef Lo weren't so incredibly nice and ridiculously modest, you would have to hate her . . ."

CUBAN CREOLE STEW
BRAISED BEEF BRISKET WITH FRESH CHORIZO AND SQUASH

Adapted from Chef Daniel Boulud's Braise: A Journey Through International Cuisine, Ecco, an imprint of HarperCollins, 2006

Serves 6–8

From French chef Daniel Boulud, this simple stew rewards you with complex taste: at once, bright, sweet, savory, zesty, spicy. If you can't find calabaza squash (aka West Indian pumpkin), substitute butternut squash, acorn squash, or pumpkin. Boulud doesn't recommend freezing.

1	(3- to 4-pound) beef brisket, trimmed
	Coarse sea salt or kosher salt
	Freshly ground black pepper
10	plum tomatoes, halved
5	cloves garlic, peeled and chopped
2	bay leaves
	Finely grated zest and freshly squeezed juice of 2 limes
1	teaspoon ground cumin
2	tablespoons extra-virgin olive oil
1	pound fresh chorizo, sliced
2	Spanish onions, peeled and chopped
3	green bell peppers, cored, seeded, and diced
1	(1-pound) calabaza squash, peeled, seeded, and cut into ½-inch dice
1	large (¾- to 1-pound) sweet potato or yam, peeled and cut into ½-inch dice
1	ripe plantain, peeled and cut into ½-inch dice
1	cup chicken stock

The day before you want to serve the dish, season the brisket with salt and pepper and place in a nonreactive container, such as a Pyrex bowl. In a blender, puree the tomatoes, garlic, bay leaves, lime zest and juice, and cumin. Pour this marinade over the brisket, allowing some to go underneath the meat. Cover tightly with plastic wrap and refrigerate overnight.

Center a rack in the oven and preheat the oven to 275°F.

Scrape the marinade off the beef, reserving the marinade. In a medium cast iron pot or Dutch oven over high heat, warm the olive oil. Add the brisket and sear both sides until golden brown, 5 to 7 minutes. Transfer the beef to a platter. Add the sausage to the pot and brown for 1 minute. Add the onions and cook until translucent, 5 to 7 minutes. Stir in the bell peppers and cook until softened, 4 to 5 minutes more.

Return the brisket to the pot. Add the reserved marinade, the squash, sweet potato, plantain, and stock. Bring to a simmer, cover, and transfer to the oven. Braise until the brisket is fork-tender, about 4 hours. Check the seasonings. If the sauce is too thin or is not flavored intensely enough, ladle most of it off into another pot and simmer it until it thickens and intensifies, then add it back to the first pot.

Transfer the brisket to a cutting board and slice the meat against the grain. Serve with the vegetables and sauce.

CORNED BEEF WITH PARSLEY SAUCE

Adapted from Colman Andrews's The Country Cooking of Ireland, *2009. Used with permission of Chronicle Books, LLC, San Francisco*

Serves 4

This is a beautiful and classic Irish dish: silken slices of corned beef are topped with a traditional shamrock green–flecked parsley sauce. Andrews makes it effortless by starting with packaged corned beef, which you can get from your butcher, order online, or find in your supermarket if you know a name to look for. Freirich is one of the most respected companies, but their presence is not, alas, national. Same with Wellshire Farms, who supplies Whole Foods with all-natural corned beef. You can order online, though, from Wellshire.

2 pounds corned beef, preferably bottom round (sometimes labeled "silverside" or brisket)

2 carrots, chopped

1 onion, chopped

2 tablespoons butter

2 tablespoons all-purpose flour

¾ cup milk

2 teaspoons minced fresh parsley

½ teaspoon English mustard

Pinch of nutmeg

Salt and pepper

Put the corned beef, carrots, and all but about 1 tablespoon of the chopped onion into a large pot, cover with water, and bring to a boil over high heat. Reduce the heat to medium-low, and skim the foam from the surface of the water. Cover and simmer for about 2½ hours, or until the corned beef is tender. Remove the beef from the liquid, wrap in foil, and set aside. Reserve about ¾ cup of the cooking liquid.

Melt the butter in a small saucepan over medium heat. Mince the reserved onion and add to the butter. Cook for about 1 minute, then whisk in the flour and cook for about 1 minute more. Add the reserved cooking liquid, the milk, parsley, mustard, nutmeg, and salt and pepper to taste, whisking the ingredients together until smooth. Cook for 5 minutes more, whisking constantly, until the sauce thickens.

To serve, slice the corned beef and spoon the sauce over it.

Admit it. You're hungry. RIGHT NOW. Richard Blais's briskety, juicy, hot, crunchy, sweet, savory burger can do that. Food porn at its finest.

Richard Blais Flips For . . .

Bravo's *Top Chef All-Stars* winner and creative director of Flip Burger in Atlanta, Richard Blais knows his burgers. He uses brisket and chuck in his favorite burger and tells us that the brisket makes it "way more juicy." His tip: Don't use a burger flattener. Let the burger shape be organic—that way it retains its juices. His take: "Brisket has a silky mouth feel to it, so it's totally worth using it." He adds, "Any way you want as far as temp is perfect. I go mid rare." He likes to serve his burger at home on a toasted brioche bun.

BRISKET BURGER

From Sam Hayward, chef and co-owner of Fore Street, Portland, Maine

Makes 4

Sam Hayward's food community consists of Maine farmers, foragers, and fishermen. Sam believes that good food travels the shortest possible distance between the farm and the table. Only local beef (for Hayward, that means from nearby Topsham) is good enough for this incredibly juicy all-brisket burger.

In a world of ground chuck and sirloin, we asked Hayward, why does he use brisket for his burgers? "In burger trials at the restaurant," says this extremely thoughtful chef, "my staff universally preferred the all-natural brisket over any other cut or combination. My family now loves this as well." He adds, "When my kids were small, they mangled the word hamburgers and called them 'hang-gibbers.' They're grown now, but still refer to them simply as 'gibbers.'"

For "gibbers" with the best taste and texture, Hayward recommends an "all-natural" brisket. The taste is intensely beefy with sweet notes and huge umami (that fifth taste, which is rich, rounded, subtle, savory, and indescribably delicious). Interestingly, he and his staff also found that the all-natural beef shrank far less when cooked, even though the fat content was nearly identical to beef from conventionally raised animals. So it's more economical, too.

If you can't grind your own brisket, ask or beg your butcher to do it for you. He or she may not have the time (or inclination) to follow the very specific instructions below, but as long as about one-fifth fat is used and the brisket is ground twice, the burgers should turn out fine anyway. So wing it if you have to—it's worth it. For Hayward's suggested roll, toppings, and condiments, see the Notes at the end of the recipe . . .

BRISKET BURGER CONTINUED . . .

About 2 pounds all-natural brisket, from the point end

Coarse sea salt

Freshly ground black pepper

Aleppo pepper

Starting with about 8 ounces of meat per person should yield about a 6-ounce patty per person. Keep the brisket very cold as you proceed. Chill the grinder parts thoroughly. Slice the thick end of the brisket across its length and against its grain into 1-inch slices. Trim some of the fat if necessary, but leave plenty in place. The objective is ground meat that is 80 percent lean, 20 percent fat. (If your brisket doesn't have enough fat, you can supplement with suet or another firm beef fat.) Cut the brisket into 1-inch cubes. Grind twice, using the medium disk. Add only as many pieces at a time as the grinder can handle without overloading.

Alternatively, trim off all the fat. Weigh the meat and fat separately, then add enough fat so that it comprises 20 percent of the total. Grind according to the previous instructions.

Gently pat the ground brisket into four 6-ounce patties, about 1 inch thick at the center. The objective is to avoid compressing and overworking the meat and to keep it slightly loose, even if the edges are not well defined and the shape seems a little crude.

Season the patties liberally on both sides with coarse sea salt, freshly ground black pepper, and a sprinkling of Aleppo pepper. Allow the patties to rest for 5 to 10 minutes before grilling or searing.

Grilling: Hayward prefers grilling over live wood embers, but the distinctive brisket flavor may be masked by smoke. As such, allow a generous charge of fruitwood, such as apple, to burn down to mostly coals with very little flame. Spread the embers evenly, heat the grill for a few minutes, then place the patties on the grill. Depending upon the temperature of the fire, cook on one side for about 5 minutes, turn once, and continue cooking on the second side for about 4 minutes to produce a warm, pink interior.

"When my kids were small, they mangled the word hamburgers and called them 'hang-gibbers.' They're grown now, but still refer to them simply as 'gibbers.'"

—*Sam Hayward, Fore Street, Portland, Maine*

Searing: Heat (but don't oil) a cast-iron skillet or griddle large enough to hold the patties without crowding. A few droplets of water splashed into the skillet should sizzle madly and vanish almost immediately. If the cast-iron is well seasoned, there may be a wisp of smoke rising from it, or heat shimmers may be visible.

Place the patties in the skillet. Cook for about 5 minutes, adjusting the temperature if necessary. Pink or watery fluid seeping onto the skillet means you may need a higher flame; excessive smoke, a lower flame. Turn and cook an additional 3 minutes or more, depending on your preference for doneness.

NOTES: If you can't find Aleppo pepper, which contributes a sweet capsicum flavor and a little spicy heat, skip it.

For the roll, Hayward prefers a classic French roll, the type made with the same dough and baking method as baguettes, with a crackling crust and an interior that can stand up to the juices released by the patties. Fork-split the rolls, open, and toast the interior surfaces slightly before using.

For toppings, really crisp romaine or redromaine leaves and slices of ripe, intense, in-season tomatoes are ideal, but don't use too many vegetables or you'll overwhelm the burger. And to get the full effect of this great meat, don't add cheese.

Hayward's preferred condiment is freshly made aïoli (he uses about one-quarter extra-virgin olive oil and three-quarters unrefined safflower oil) finished with fresh tomato that has been squeezed, chopped, sautéed, and reduced to a thick consistency in a skillet with a little olive oil and a splash of white wine vinegar. (Fold the tomato mixture into the aïoli after it's cooled down.)

Sam Hayward in the open kitchen of his restaurant, only blocks from the water, in food-centric Portland, Maine. Trust me, the freshest fish go to Sam.

FATTY 'CUE'S
AWARD-WINNING SWEET CHILI JAM

Adapted from a recipe by Zak Pelaccio and Robbie Richter of Fatty 'Cue, Brooklyn, New York

Makes about 1 pint

Here is the secret to the brisket sandwich New York Magazine *called "fiendishly good" when they named it Sandwich of the Year in 2009. Sam Sifton, reviewing it in the* New York Times: *"Deckle deliciousness from psychedelic Texas." This sandwich's sauce—"so thick it's more like jam," says Fatty 'Cue's pit master Robbie Richter—is way more than a supporting player. We have adapted it to the closest possible approximation. But if you don't feel like going on a scavenger hunt for ingredients, just set your GPS for 91 South 6th Street in trendoid Williamsburg, Brooklyn. And don't expect it at dinner. Their brisket sandwich is only on their lunch and late night menus.*

2	tablespoons canola oil
1	cup sliced shallots
½	cup destemmed, seeded, and sliced long red chiles
¼	cup sliced garlic
¼	cup peeled and sliced galangal (see Notes)
⅛	cup dried shrimp
¼	cup palm sugar (see Notes)
¼	cup smoked tomatoes, peeled and seeded (see Notes)
⅛	cup tamarind (see Notes)
¼	teaspoon belacan, toasted (see Notes)
⅛	cup fish sauce

Heat the oil in a large sauté pan over medium heat, then add the shallots, chiles, garlic, galangal, and the dried shrimp. Cook, stirring occasionally, until fragrant and slightly softened, about 5 minutes. Remove the mixture to a small bowl lined with a paper towel and set aside.

Wash the pan, then add the palm sugar and smoked tomatoes and turn the heat to medium. When the palm sugar has dissolved, add the tamarind and belacan and cook for 2 to 3 minutes, stirring occasionally. If the mixture starts to burn or gets really thick, simply reduce the heat.

Stir in the reserved shallot mixture and cook until warmed through. Allow the mixture to cool slightly in the pan, then purée in a blender or food processor. Stir in the fish sauce. The chile jam keeps in a tightly covered container in the refrigerator for about 1 week.

Robbie Richter: "You can dilute this jam with water . . . You can put a dollop on a piece of smoked brisket . . . You can easily use it on chicken or steak or just about any other meat."

Me: "Frankly, you could probably slather it on a stale Twinkie and feel the earth move."

NOTES: Look for Asian ingredients in Asian food shops or the international section of your supermarket.

Galangal, a rhizome, is a member of the ginger family. If you can't find it, substitute ginger, although galangal doesn't really have the same peppery heat.

Belacan, or shrimp paste, is made from fermented shrimp and is extremely pungent. To toast it, compress it into a disk and wrap in a small piece of aluminum foil. Hold it over a gas burner for about 30 to 60 seconds per side. Properly toasted belacan will be lightly browned and crisp around the edges. The toasting will also cause a strong smoky burning smell that will linger and seep into your clothes, so be sure to turn on the exhaust fan and open the windows during the process.

If you can't find palm sugar, substitute brown sugar, although it won't have the same complex flavor.

For tamarind (which lends a sour note to dishes), when starting with tamarind paste, steep a little in hot water for about 10 minutes, then mash thoroughly and push the mixture through a sieve. Use the resulting juicy pulp and discard the bits of seed and pod.

If you don't want to smoke your own tomatoes, use Muir Glen's Fire-Roasted Diced Tomatoes, discarding the juice.

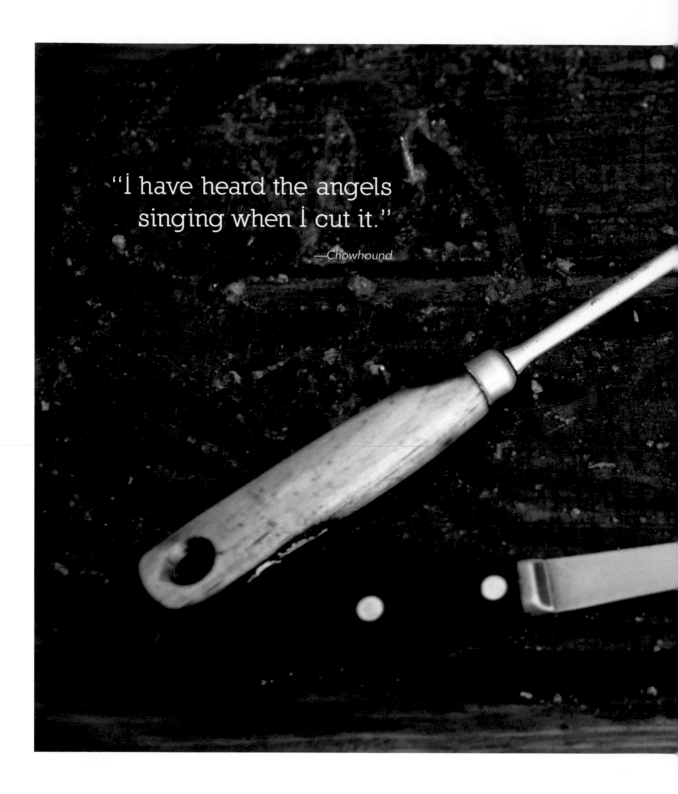

"I have heard the angels singing when I cut it."

—*Chowhound*

Sunny yellow it is at Cook's Illustrated—on the plate and on the tie.

8 In Which Chris Kimball Interrogates a Brisket. (Chris Wins.)

"With Chris Kimball, if it isn't perfection, it isn't progress."

Whether it's in print, online, or on television, whether it's for grating zucchini, making a carbonnade à la flamande, or cooking a brisket, *Cook's Illustrated* gives you the what, the why, the why not, the how-to, the science, the tried, the true, the tested, the template. I always knew that *Cook's Illustrated* had high standards but until I actually paid them a visit, I had no idea just how high they were. Old-fashioned words like thorough and rigorous leap to mind. Frankly, after just five minutes in their test kitchen, I understood why a number of their cookbooks have Best or Bible in their titles. And while someone like Oprah may say, "Progress, not perfection," this new-age forgiveness mantra is not for *Cook's Illustrated* founder, publisher, editor Chris Kimball. If it isn't perfection, it isn't progress.

The goal at *Cook's Illustrated* is to fashion a recipe so clear and precise that anyone can make it successfully. Thanks to Mr. Kimball and a staff equally obsessed with perfection, no scone is left unturned. "Might they need to try 500 batches of chocolate pudding? They will. Selflessly," notes an awed online fan. "Could we defy 100 years of French culinary tradition and create an omelet you could get right the first time?" they ask themselves? What do you think?! Another area of stunning overachievement is "Problem/Solution." At *Cook's Illustrated*, they often solve problems you didn't even know you had. I personally never worried about why "the berry flavor in blueberry muffins is fleeting." Or wondered why "flank steak stuffing won't stay put." Or fretted that the wrong vegetable peeler leads to hand strain.

Thank God they could worry for me.

"Every time I see one of their recipes specifying something like '6/17ths' of a teaspoon, all I can think is 'Oh puhleeze!'"

—*Chowhound*

And now I'm facing a private five-hour brisket cooking tutorial in their test kitchen (aka America's Test Kitchen, often shortened to ATK) in the upscale Starbuckian village of Brookline, Massachusetts, a short cab ride from Boston. If you like antiques, yarn, old-fashioned candy, you will love ambling around leafy Brookline. The day of my visit, my cabdriver got hopelessly lost. We must have passed the Children's Bookshop four times before we found it: *Cook's Illustrated*'s headquarters is in what looks like a once prosperous old New England factory building, all aged red brick, period wrought iron winding staircase, and for a company that likes to make a splash, almost no signage.

But up on the second floor, more than three dozen full-time cooks and food testers fine-tune recipes, tweaking each technique and ingredient up to seventy times for each dish over a period of a month or more. The final recipes are then sent out to 2,000 volunteer home cooks who are asked to fill out a survey essentially saying yea or nay. If a recipe raises any questions, the ATK often turns for advice to a food chemist like Guy Crosby, who has a doctorate in organic chemistry, more than thirty years of experience in food science, and who teaches at—where else?—Harvard.

More about the kitchen, which is huge—2,500 square feet, handsome, and recently renovated. Light streams through large windows. Shining stainless-steel counters hold all the carefully prepped and measured ingredients, neatly lined up at work stations. There are conveniently placed banks of ovens and stovetops to make everything easier. True to their belief that everything needs to be accessible to home cooks, everything in the kitchen is top-notch, but nothing is fancy or Euro-fab.

Test kitchen director Erin McMurrer prepares the onions for their entrance.

Slicing the brisket into just-so quarter-inch slices and removing excess fat. But keep those juices coming!

It's the vibe in the kitchen that is even more impressive. The day that I am there, everyone is outfitted in identical crisp white chefy jackets with neat white toggle buttons. There's a quiet hum of activity, focus, and purpose—no wasted movement and for these professionals, no distraction from the task at hand. Just think the exact opposite of any episode of *Top Chef.* No one drops a pan or burns the butter or screams, "Oh, fuck! What's wrong with the fucking timer on this fucking convection oven?!" You get the feeling that if an alien spaceship landed in the center of the test kitchen, someone would just pause, quietly text 911, then get back to testing a BLT.

Chris Kimball is the very public face of this culinary empire. His patrician New England looks (almost always a crisp bow tie in place) and preppy demeanor don't quite jibe with the folksy/geeky manner he presents in his magazine columns or on his television show. In fact, the moment I shook hands with him, post-brisket, I thought someone this determinedly friendly just cannot really be so cozy comfortable with people. Later, I saw a piece from a Boston newspaper that noted, "Kimball has been known to make test-kitchen chefs and writers cry with his scathing criticisms."

But Chris Kimball's enthusiasm for how to get the world to eat better food is genuine. And if he profits financially from that, more power to him. He is one incredible businessman. If you could buy stock—and I do not mean chicken—in his company (alas, it's still private), buy some shares of Mr. Kimball. The *Boston Globe* noted, "Kitchen stickler Christopher Kimball, creator of *America's Test Kitchen* and *Cook's Illustrated*, has built a company that is thriving even as the media industry collapses like an undercooked soufflé." Their rough estimate (in 2009) was that the gross revenue for print and Web subscriptions alone was more than $40 million a year. That's a whole lot of never overkneaded dough!

> "If you find yourself serving tough meat, what did you do wrong? You were impatient. Just put the bloody thing back on the stove and cook until it's fork-tender."
>
> —*Chris Kimball*

Cook's Illustrated
A BETTER WAY TO COOK BRISKET

1. Use a Dutch oven or cast-iron skillet to weight the meat down as it browns.

2. Carefully pour the sauce and onions into a foil-lined baking dish.

3. Place the brisket on top of the sauce, fat side up, nestling the meat into the liquid and onions.

4. Fold the flaps of foil to wrap the brisket securely, but do not wrap it too tightly.

In addition to his other jobs, he oversees *Cook's Country* magazine, produces hefty cookbooks (perfect wedding presents, believers rave), a huge *Cook's Illustrated* "community" Web presence, the most popular cooking show on public television with an estimated 2,000,000 viewers. Mr. Kimball has his own books (the latest, well-reviewed *Fannie's Last Supper: Re-creating One Amazing Meal from Fannie Farmer's 1896 Cookbook*), a new radio show featuring guess-who, and yet another magazine, *Entertaining from Cook's Illustrated*.

To Mr. Kimball's credit, his enterprises don't just have readers, subscribers, fans—they have believers. It's almost a cult. "I was always a decent cook, but after finding *Cook's Illustrated* I became an amazing cook," someone confides to Amazon. "The bible of cooking perfection," raves the *Dallas Morning News*. From a cultish member on prudentbaby.com: "Because of what I've learned from ATK, I feel fully confident to go into the kitchen with nothing but beans, rice, an onion, and some garlic and the dinner will be simple but delicious." "A reason to turn on the stove again," enthuses the *Omaha World-Herald*, leading one to wonder whether it was all take-out pizza and frozen Hot Pockets in Nebraska until someone discovered The World According to Chris Kimball.

What doesn't *Cook's Illustrated* do well? To be sure, not everyone is convinced that the obsessively examined cooking system is the way to go. A Chowhound reader admits to a conflicted love/hate relationship: "Every time I see a recipe specifying something like '6/17ths' of a teaspoon, all I can think is, 'Oh puhleeze!'" And an online detractor believes their desire to perfect recipes "seems to suck the joy and love out of cooking." Ouch!

Well, joy, love, and brisket were in abundance that golden autumn day when I finally found my way up the stairs to that test kitchen. Erin McMurrer, the test kitchen's director, was about to teach me how to make the perfect brisket. While it is clear from the moment you meet her that she is experienced and confident, Ms. McMurrer is also incredibly patient and kind. She reminds me of Mrs. Angela Piper, my first grade teacher, who never made me feel stupid about coloring the sky chartreuse and purple. You don't have to take my word for it: see for yourself on one of their television shows. While Mr. Kimball analyzes, holds forth, and sort of jokes with colleagues, Ms. McMurrer just kind of radiates quiet competence and good cheer.

And so the lesson begins. Me, Ms. McMurrer, a brisket. Mr. Kimball would join us later. Our recipe was first published in 2005 and takes everything into consideration, not least of which is what *Cook's Illustrated* calls the "all-too-common problem of a brisket turning out to be dry and chewy."

"Dry and chewy" are not in Ms. McMurrer's vocabulary. Neither is "problem." Here's the recipe for what proved to be a juicy plateful of heaven in Brookline Village:

A perfectly perfect brisket. In the words of *Cook's Illustrated*.

ONION-BRAISED BEEF BRISKET

Cook's Illustrated, *Published January 1, 2005*

Serves 6–8

This recipe requires a few hours of unattended cooking. It also requires advance preparation. After cooking, the brisket must stand overnight in the braising liquid that later becomes the sauce; this helps to keep the brisket moist and flavorful. Defatting the sauce is essential. If the fat has congealed into a layer on top of the sauce, it can be easily removed while cold. Sometimes, however, fragments of solid fat are dispersed throughout the sauce; in this case, the sauce should be skimmed of fat after reheating. If you prefer a spicy sauce, increase the amount of cayenne to ¼ teaspoon from ⅛ teaspoon. You will need 18-inch-wide heavy-duty foil for this recipe. If you own an electric knife, it will make easy work of slicing the cold brisket.

1   **beef brisket, 4 to 5 pounds, flat cut preferred**

   Vegetable oil

3   **large onions (about 2½ pounds), halved and sliced ½ inch thick**

1   **tablespoon brown sugar**

3   **medium cloves garlic, minced or pressed through garlic press (about 1 tablespoon)**

1   **tablespoon tomato paste**

1   **tablespoon paprika**

⅛   **teaspoon cayenne pepper**

2   **tablespoons all-purpose flour**

1   **cup low-sodium chicken broth**

1   **cup dry red wine**

3   **bay leaves**

3   **sprigs fresh thyme**

2   **teaspoons cider vinegar (to season sauce before serving)**

Adjust the oven rack to the lower middle position; preheat the oven to 300°F.

Line a 13- by 9-inch baking dish with two 24-inch-long sheets of 18-inch-wide heavy-duty aluminum foil, positioning the sheets perpendicular to each other and allowing the excess foil to extend beyond the edges of the pan. Pat the brisket dry with paper towels. Place the brisket fat side up on a cutting board; using a dinner fork, poke holes in the meat through the fat layer about 1 inch apart. Season both sides of the brisket liberally with salt and pepper.

Heat 1 teaspoon oil in a 12-inch skillet over medium-high heat until the oil just begins to smoke. Place the brisket fat side up in the skillet (the brisket may climb up the sides of the skillet); weight the brisket with a heavy Dutch oven or cast-iron skillet and cook until well browned, about 7 minutes. Remove the Dutch oven; using tongs, flip the brisket and cook on the second side without weight until well browned, about 7 minutes longer. Transfer the brisket to a platter.

Pour off all but 1 tablespoon fat from the pan (or, if the brisket was lean, add enough oil to the fat in the skillet to equal 1 tablespoon); stir in the onions, sugar, and ¼ teaspoon salt and cook over medium-high heat, stirring occasionally, until the onions are softened and golden, 10 to 12 minutes. Add the garlic and cook, stirring frequently, until fragrant, about 1 minute; add the tomato paste and cook, stirring to combine, until the paste darkens, about 2 minutes. Add the paprika and cayenne and cook, stirring constantly, until fragrant, about 1 minute. Sprinkle the flour over the onions and cook, stirring constantly, until well combined, about 2 minutes. Add the broth, wine, bay leaves, and thyme, stirring to scrape up browned bits from the pan; bring to a simmer and simmer for about 5 minutes to fully thicken.

Pour the sauce and onions into the foil-lined baking dish. Nestle the brisket, fat side up, in the sauce and onions. Fold the foil extensions over and seal (do not tightly crimp the foil because the foil must later be opened to test for doneness). Place in the oven and cook until a fork can be inserted into and removed from the center of the brisket with no resistance, 3½ to 4 hours (when testing for doneness, open the foil with caution as the contents will be steaming). Carefully open the foil and let the brisket cool at room temperature for 20 to 30 minutes.

Transfer the brisket to a large bowl; set a mesh strainer over the bowl and strain the sauce over the brisket. Discard the bay leaves and thyme from the onions and transfer the onions to a small bowl. Cover both bowls with plastic wrap, cut vents in the plastic with a paring knife, and refrigerate overnight.

About 45 minutes before serving, adjust the oven rack to the lower middle position; preheat the oven to 350°F.

While the oven heats, transfer the cold brisket to a cutting board. Scrape off and discard any congealed fat from the sauce, then transfer the sauce to a medium saucepan and heat over medium heat until warm, skimming any fat on the surface with a wide shallow spoon (you should have about 2 cups of sauce without onions; if necessary, simmer the sauce over medium-high heat until reduced to 2 cups). While the sauce heats, use a chef's or carving knife to slice the brisket against the grain into ¼-inch-thick slices, trimming and discarding any excess fat, if desired; place the slices in a 13- by 9-inch baking dish. Stir the reserved onions and vinegar into the warmed sauce and adjust the seasoning with salt and pepper. Pour the sauce over the brisket slices, cover the baking dish with foil, and bake until heated through, 25 to 30 minutes. Serve immediately.

Left: Putting the onions through their paces.
Right: It's a tough job, but someone's gotta do it.

And what else did I, a seeker of perfect brisket, learn by asking Erin questions that day? (And, full disclosure, acting as if I knew the answers all along.)

ME: "I know you cook your brisket the day before. Do you have to bring the meat to room temp before you pop it in the oven?"

ERIN: "It doesn't need to be room temperature. We've found that if you put the brisket out for an hour, it only goes up 7 degrees. So we put it in the oven straight from the refrigerator."

Author's note (NEWS BULLETIN): If nothing else in this entire book will knock the socks off your know-it-all foodie friends, the fact that the meat doesn't need to be room temperature will. Drop that at your next dinner party!!!

ME: "What cut do you use?"

ERIN: "We use the brisket flat—just because it's more available to home cooks."

ME: "In Step One, why do you prick the meat with a fork?"

ERIN: "Using a dinner fork to prick it helps the fat render out."

ME: "What kind of broth would you recommend?"

ERIN: "We use low-sodium because high-sodium can get too salty as it cooks down."

ME: "Why so much stirring?"

ERIN: "You deglaze the pan and scrape up all the stuff on the bottom, called the 'fond.' The 'fond' is browned bits of protein."

ME: "I knew that." (No, I didn't.)

ME: "Why do you need the foil?"

ERIN: "The foil obviously helps to seal. It also forces the liquid to stay close to the brisket so the sauce will come out more concentrated. Start out with less liquid and it's already more concentrated."

ME: "What kind of wine do you use?"

ERIN: "A Côtes du Rhône. It's medium-bodied, full flavored, slightly fruity, not too expensive."

ME: "Most recipes don't use flour. Why does yours?"

ERIN: "Flour thickens the sauce. Better clingability."

(I'm thinking. "Is 'clingability' a word? It should be a word.")

ME: "How thick to slice?"

ERIN: "I'd say ¼-inch slices."

ME: "Why is it so much better to cook the night before?"

ERIN: "Because the brisket absorbs all the juice. And you can easily take out the fat. Brisket is cooperative if you cool it overnight." (To prove this point, we cooked one brisket from scratch, but actually ate an immensely cooperative reheated brisket that Erin had fully cooked the night before.)

ME: "Why the vinegar?"

ERIN: "The vinegar brightens the sauce. You just don't need to add too much for that to happen."

ME: "How do you know if you're slicing it against the grain?"

ERIN: "Make a slice to see that you're right. If I cut it with the grain, it will be stringy and not very good. What I'm doing by cutting against the grain is shortening the long strands so it is more tender."

ME: "I'm starving!!!!!!!!"

At this point, Chris Kimball comes down to meet with us and have a taste. "Is this the ultimate stop on the brisket highway?" he asks. Actually, it pretty much was. I had a few questions for him.

ME: "Advice to brides?"

CHRIS: "Just cook the brisket until it's tender. And defat it properly. It's really about the sauce, isn't it? Anyone can make a brisket . . . simmer for three hours and you're done."

ME: "Why brisket? What makes it so special?"

CHRIS: "It's the ultimate mom/grandma recipe. Something you grew up with. It has taste memories. It's also a very personal recipe—unlike sugar cookies or oatmeal cookies, the taste difference between brisket recipes is huge."

And this, not from our interview, but from Mr. Kimball's excellent book, *The Kitchen Detective*: "If you find yourself serving tough meat, what did you do wrong? You were impatient. Just put the bloody thing back on the stove and cook until it's fork-tender."

But how does it taste? It tastes ambrosial. It is so glorious, with deep tastes colliding in your mouth: bright hits of vinegar infused with sweet onion essence and hints of dusky paprika and fruity wine. You cannot not make a perfect brisket with Erin McMurrer and Chris Kimball. If you do, you have only yourself to blame.

The brisket sandwich (inexplicably named "The Mary Ann") at Slows in Detroit. How does Niman Ranch brisket, chopped and served with a tangy smokehouse sauce, sound to you? I thought so.

9 Brisket Has Many Sides: What Goes with It

> "I didn't claw my way to the top of the food chain to become a vegetarian."
>
> —*The Kansas City Barbeque Society Cookbook*

BARBECUED BRISKET

"There is room for all God's creatures, right next to the potato salad and the coleslaw." If you are a barbecued brisket lover, could you say it with any more grace than pickledpigs.com? So, let there be potato salad and coleslaw. But during my extensive study of brisket side dishes, what I wanted to know was—aside from potato salad and slaw—what else would/should a typical barbecue place have? And is there a typical barbecue place? How is what you serve at home different? If you make a traditional braised brisket, do you keep the side dishes traditional? And why does so little green appear on any brisket plate anywhere? Oh, and what's with those slabs of white bread that you get at those 'cue joints? (I've done so much researching and writing by now that I am finally able to say " 'cue" joint without feeling like a character out of *Fried Green Tomatoes*. Which in itself happens to be a popular barbecue side dish!)

In no particular order: First, the lack of side dishes altogether in some well-known barbecue places. Unless you count pickles. Which also seem to count as a vegetable. No barbecue sauce either. Does it bother people? It doesn't seem to. A stalwart on Chowhound: "I don't go for a well-rounded meal with sides and a dessert. I go for the meat." A Texas barbecue festival announces: "Because most people can't live on brisket alone, we are providing booth space for other food vendors to sell their items." Note the *most people*. It sounds kind of begrudging to me, like *better people* can live on brisket alone.

> "You don't get fancy with barbecue. When you get fancy, you get out of line."
>
> —*Barbecue legend Arthur Bryant*

Robb Walsh, whose barbecue focus and expertise is Texas, gives an interesting reason in *Legends of Texas Barbecue* why some barbecue places don't offer a lot of sides: some barbecue places in Texas remain the butcher shops they began as. They're not really restaurants. "To this day," he says, "they offer barbecue the way farm workers ate it—with no plates, no knives, no forks—just a slab of meat on a piece of butcher paper." At Kreuz (the locals pronounce it "Krites") in Lockhart, Texas (barbecue capital of the world), it's really more grocery food than side dish: they will serve you slices of orange cheese, fresh tomato, avocados, onion chunks.

No matter where you devour your plateful of steaming hot smoked brisket, you can pretty much count on the fact that there won't be a wine list, valet parking, linen napkins. At B. B.'s Lawnside BBQ in Kansas City, there's not only no lawn, there's very little dishwashing. Everything's served in Styrofoam bowls and plastic baskets. To quote the late Arthur Bryant, the King of Kansas City smoking and Calvin Trillin's onetime hero, "You don't get fancy with barbecue. When you

. . . And on your left, spaghetti tossed in sweetened barbecue sauce and chopped smoked brisket. This bliss from The Bar-B-Q Shop in Memphis, Tennessee.

get fancy, you get out of line." "Meathead"of AmazingRibs.com embraces it all: "If you don't get it on your shirt you're not doing it right." He also gives a snarky smack to Kansas Citians, telling me that he serves his brisket, Texas-style, "with only a few spoons of a thin, tart, tomato soup–like sauce, none of that thick sweet Kansas City stuff." As if he hasn't made his point, he adds, "Brisket needs sugar like steers need wolves."

So . . . the point is that barbecue is essentially an unapologetically cheerful, opinionated meatcentric mess. "The conventional wisdom," according to food critics Rob Patronite and Robin Raisfeld, "is the better the barbecue, the worse the sides." What can you expect in most barbecue places? Potatoes, pretty much, always and everywhere. Whether it's French fries (double-fried in lard at Arthur Bryant's in Kansas City), sweet potato fries, potato salad. Beans—from baked beans to apple baked beans to bean salads. Coleslaw. Then there are the regional and seasonal specialties: collard

Brisket cinephiles: catch the captivating homemade video "Mutton by Moonlite" on YouTube.

The Better the 'Cue, the Worse the Sides?

Nationally or regionally, there's a lot of just plain not-at-all plain specialties that disprove a theory that the better the 'cue, the worse the sides: the rich sweet potato casserole from Melvin's Legendary Bar-B-Q in Mount Pleasant, South Carolina; Stone Ale chili cheese fries from The Beach Pit BBQ in Costa Mesa, California; deep-smoked corn at Stacy's Smokehouse BBQ in Phoenix, Arizona; rum baked beans from Fat Matt's Rib Shack in Atlanta, Georgia; a crunchy Tater Tot casserole from Opie's Barbecue in Spicewood, Texas; sweet fresh-baked corn bread muffins at Famous Dave's (a 'cue franchise, serving ambrosial muffins in thirty-six states); a thick homestyle burgoo at Moonlite Bar-B-Q Inn in Owensboro, Kentucky (they're cooking cinematically, too—catch their captivating homemade YouTube video, "Mutton by Moonlite.") Off the beaten (biscuit) track, there's a food truck in New Orleans, Uncle Lee-Bird's Boo Koo BBQ, that gets online raves. "They're kicking it up with BBQ pulled pork with blue cheese and cilantro coleslaw, boudin beignets, pulled pork egg rolls, and crawfish-stuffed pistolettes!"

Vibrant mashed sweet potatoes vie with warm bourbon-drenched peaches and golden mac and cheese for your favorite side dish. From the takeout counter at Daisy May's BBQ in New York City.

Counter-clockwise from top: Yes, they're shaped like golden halos. Heavenly onion rings from Johnny's BBQ, Mission, Kansas. Crispy Asian-fusion sautéed green beans. A baked potato filled with chopped brisket burnt ends, topped with cheese, sour cream, and chives—"Honey, we're going to Fiorella's Jack Stack Barbecue in Kansas City, Missouri, tonight!"

greens, hush puppies, Brunswick stew, black-eyed peas down South; German potato salad, pinto beans, fried okra, Texas toast in Texas; cheesy corn and red hot chile peppers in Kansas City. Corn on the cob in the summer, sometimes grilled. Chili in the winter. (This seems like a good time to let you in on one of the best—and most toe-tapping, knee-slapping ways to learn about regional barbecue. It's "The BBQ Song" with Rhett & Link & The Homestead Pickers and you can find it on YouTube where it's had more than a million hits. Don't you wish you'd written the lyric, "When my life is through . . . bury me in barbecue.")

Barbecuing at home and entertaining friends? Anything goes and it goes beyond a handful of fries and a scoop of coleslaw. Here's what you'd get at Ardie Davis's house in Kansas City: "I usually serve warm mildly spicy pinto beans or barbecue beans (barbecued rib scraps, sautéed onions and peppers, sweet barbecue sauce, canned pork and beans, rinsed—slow simmered in the oven for a minimum of 45 minutes at 225° to 250°F), plus pan-fried potatoes and coleslaw. If Texans are present I add pickled jalapeño peppers and saltine crackers on the side and serve pinto beans instead of barbecue beans. Bread, eight-grain or cheap sandwich bread, is available, but I want the meat to be so tasty that guests won't want bread." And what's up with the bread? Barbecue is traditionally served on a slice of white bread. From *Saveur*, with snark: "Sopping up barbecue may well be the only legitimate use for spongy, store-bought white bread." Well, besides making a sandwich. When I went to barbecue places for the fabulous food-tasting portion of this show, I realized you don't just say "hold the bread." You just get it on your plate because it's what they do. When in Rome . . . Georgia . . .

Finally, the lack of greens. This holds true for barbecued and for braised briskets, too. Whenever anyone talked to me about any kind of brisket, they never said: "Oh, and I served it with green beans and almonds." Or "Everyone loved the stir-fried broccoli." And here's why: brisket is simply not about green vegetables. Seriously not. I came across a back and forth online where some guy said he mentioned to his friends that he was thinking of requesting a salad to go with his barbecue lunch. "You would have thought I suggested serving monkey meat in its own scull."

Braised Brisket

While there's slightly less stigma for the braised brisket home cook, there's not much vegetable love here either. "It's a mushy experience, and you want to keep it that way," says my friend, Lois. Lois cooks brisket all year-round and says that she does conscientiously shop for greenmarket vegetables to serve with it, but I could tell that what she really wanted to talk about was her double-baked potatoes.

Most brisket pros hold that the perfect side dish for a braised brisket must meet two criteria: it has to be a crowd pleaser and it has to be something that functions as a gravy picker up. Welcome, potatoes or noodles. "What does a good brisket need as a side dish?" I asked my boyfriend, who grew up with brisket. "Potatoes," he said. "Noodles." He paused, then added, "Starch, starch, more starch." So my boyfriend and Chris Kimball have at least one thing in common. For their Onion-Braised Beef Brisket (page 158), *Cook's Illustrated* suggests that "good accompaniments to braised brisket include mashed potatoes and egg noodles."

"When asked why he got into the barbecue business, Kansas City 'cue chef Lindsay Shannon says, 'I was half-crazy, and I wanted to be all-the-way crazy.'"

—*Saveur*

Left: Fresh broccoli with garlic. Yes, it's green. But that doesn't make it bad. Traditional Jewish barley and mushrooms. Top right: A hearty side dish of kasha varnishkes, featuring slightly chewy bow-tie noodles, possibly the only thing al dente in the entire brisket universe. Bottom right: Noodle kugel, moist on the inside and crisp on the outside. This is where words like "bubbie" come up.

"Brisket is a real family and friends meal. It's not something you'd serve at a *grand déjeuner*."

—Nach Waxman

If you're not in the mood for mashed potatoes, the number-one fan favorite, how about smashed, baked, or oven-roasted? How about red potatoes, purple potatoes, new potatoes, sweet potatoes? Potato blintzes, potato kugels, or potato latkes? Going a little fancier? There's potato purée and potatoes au gratin. And don't forget the plump and happy gravy-infused wedges of Idaho potatoes that get to simmer in the pot alongside your brisket. (What you will not find ever with a traditional, homemade braised brisket is potato salad or French fries.)

Moving on to noodles. Noodles can be simple, sweet, savory, narrow, broad. Everything from basic buttered egg noodles (as quick to cook as brisket is slow) to pappardelle (check out the poetically named Pasta Ribbons with Shredded Beef Brisket on Epicurious) to noodle pudding. Not to mention everyone's favorite noodle dish: kasha varnishkes—the traditional combination of buckwheat groats (Healthy!), onions, and bow tie pasta, served with a big spoon and a whole lot of nostalgia. This is the dish where people say, "Oh, my bubbe made this." And you can make it more easily than your bubbe. Food maven, cookbook author, and restaurant critic Arthur Schwartz says to just follow the directions on the back of the kasha box. Then top each helping with onions and juices from the meat. (One of the biggest brands is Wolff's Kasha.)

Basically, the thinking goes, make anything that adds joy and more comfort to what is already comfort food. A family side dish to go with what is the family main dish. Whatever you grew up with. Something as fork-tender and scrumptious as the brisket itself.

Vegetables, meh. You can't go wrong with roasted root vegetables in winter, green beans in summer, spinach and broccoli all year long. Unless you're one of the few big deal restaurant chefs serving braised brisket, in which case you would want to go a little more pyrotechnical with the starch, vegetable, and salad since you're not serving fifteen people, one of whom is your ten-year-old second cousin, Eloise, one of the pickiest eaters in Winnetka, Illinois. At home, traditional—or at least known—is never a bad thing. Brisket isn't looking for a chic new vegetable sidekick like a Lady Godiva squash or Turkish orange eggplant. It wouldn't know what to do with crispy basil fried rice. Well, Anita Lo would know.

It isn't that you can't change anything about a beloved family brisket. It's just that why would you? But (I know you) if you do decide to go where no one in your clan has gone before, making polenta or orzo rather than noodles, say, or fresh braised rhubarb instead of broccoli, just know that it's easier (and less traumatic) to alter the side dish than it is to tamper with the main dish. Take note of what gifted cook Dan Palmer (page 92) told me, "One year, I said, 'Oh, I've been making this forever. I'll try another recipe.' I think I tried a *Barefoot Contessa* brisket. People were very upset and said, 'Never do that again!' That was the one and only time I strayed. Never again!"

In Simon Hopkinson's *Second Helpings of Roast Chicken*, he mourns the loss of the traditional brisket places he loved in London but finds a spot of hope in the fact that, just across the channel, Parisian bistros still manage to seduce patrons with exquisite plates of simply boiled beef and carrots. You can almost hear Hopkinson sigh as he writes: "Yet it is surely a comfort to know that somewhere, not too far away, convention remains a finer thing than fashion, perceived expediency, and, above all, complacency on the part of the consumer."

Dan Palmer's brisket 1997

Dan Palmer's brisket 2004

Dan Palmer's brisket 2011

Even straight out of the can, jellied cranberry orbs are satiny, smooth, and sweetly satisfying.

What Goes?

What do the very best brisket makers serve with their own briskets?

Temple Emanu-El Brisket (p. 91)
Serve with mashed potatoes, kugel, and some kind of vegetable.

My Favorite Brisket (p. 105)
Serve with farfel (boiled egg barley noodles), noodle kugel, or potato pancakes. A colorful winter salad goes well with this.

Braised Fresh Brisket in Stout with Onions (p. 126)
Chef Hopkinson suggests accompanying this with either plainly boiled or creamed potatoes.

Aunt Gladys's Brisket (p. 92)
Serve it with kasha varnishkes and a seasonal vegetable. It can also be served as leftovers, reheated on challah, or as an open-faced sandwich.

Classic Braised Beef Brisket (p. 125)
Chef Gray serves it with roasted baby turnips and fingerling potatoes.

Slow Cooker Brisket (p. 97)
Serve with a couple of the following: baked beans, scalloped or baked potatoes, green beans, salad, garlic bread, you name it.

Barbecued Brisket Sandwiches (with Firecracker Sauce) (p. 132)
Chef Page serves this on potato rolls as a sandwich, but it would also be fine alone with side dishes like potato salad and coleslaw.

Sephardic Brisket (p. 134)
Serve with saffron rice, mashed potatoes, or couscous.

Nach Waxman's Brisket of Beef (p. 110)
Sauerkraut (ideally homemade) is perfect. Potato dumplings or potato pancakes are great accompaniments. Some folks like applesauce on the side.

Beef Brisket with Tangy Peaches (p. 131)
Chef Shields suggests that for a nice change from the usual brisket and potato combo, try serving the brisket with some cheese grits (American polenta).

Barbecue Green Chile Brisket (p. 124)
Chef Baum serves this on its own with corn bread or tortillas; in a burrito; on chile cheese dogs or French fries; on top of a baked potato with cheese.

SHREDDED BRISKET
W/KETCHUP

ARDIE'S BBQ BRISKET

brisket ragu

brisket ragu

brisket w/carrots

BRISKET SOUP
FOR NATE

Brisket w/onions

"I thought only God could invent something as good as a brisket taco."

—*Dallas restaurant critic Leslie Brenner*

No Brisket Left Behind

What to do with leftovers (Hint: slice, shred, pull apart, cube, freeze, reheat)

- Brisket soups
- Brisket po'boys
- Brisket tacos
- Brisket sandwiches
- Brisket burritos
- Brisket hash
- Brisket enchiladas
- Brisket potpies
- Brisket on yellow rice and black beans with chopped onion and grated cheese
- Brisket sloppy joes
- Brisket sandwiches
- Brisket mixed with barbecue sauce and sweet onions; place on hamburger buns
- Smoked brisket chili
- Brisket omelet
- Cheesy baked potato with shredded brisket
- Pinto beans with brisket
- Brisket pasta sauce
- Cold, on the kitchen counter, with beer

Chateau Brisket

2011 Reserve

10 Cheers!
What to Drink with Brisket.

"Big flavor demands a big wine. A robust beer. A sidecar."

Well, occasionally it has gentle notes and feminine cues, but all you have to do is look at the kind of POW! things that go into a full-force brisket (soy sauce, black tea, powdered mace, mole sauce) and things that go on a brisket (chili powder, jalapeño powder, cayenne, mustard powder) to know that you're not going to be sipping a delicate rosé with it.

Brisket, with all due respect, is not particularly in touch with its feminine side. You know those dopey Facebook quizzes? Well, if brisket was a magazine, it would be *Maxim*. If it was an actor, it would be Daniel Craig. If it was a television show, it would be *Ice Road Truckers*.

So when I interviewed brewmasters, brewery owners, mixologists, and wine experts, none of them suggested Perrier as a pairing. What I did get from everyone I talked to—besides some really specific pitch-perfect combinations—were some pairing ground rules.

ONE: Big flavor demands a big wine. A robust beer. A sidecar.

TWO: Whether it's beer, wine, or hard liquor, you want something that harmonizes with the brisket or you want something that contrasts or plays off it.

THREE: Brisket may be more "Downstairs" than "Upstairs," but don't rule out something sparkling: a Prosecco or a Cava. Or méthode champenoise beers. Especially if you're celebrating something. Or maybe you and your entire family lost all your savings to a Ponzi scheme and need something with some happy bubbles.

FOUR: Why not enjoy the same wine your brisket is enjoying? Malbec in your brisket . . . Malbec in your wineglass. It matches stylistically.

FIVE: Bring out the specificity. A spicy brisket deserves nothing less than a spicy counterpart. Craft Restaurant's head mixologist Sean McClure's aptly named cocktail, Clove'N Hoof (read down . . . bottoms up!), actually has cloves in it.

SIX: Smoke goes with smoke. This is true for cocktails, says Sean McClure. A smoky Scotch with a smoky barbecue. Bacon-infused bourbon, suggests mixologist Brian Van Flandern, who heads up a creative cocktail consultancy, mymixologist.com.

SEVEN: Yes to Liquid Smoke. A bartender told me that he had recently used Liquid Smoke in a tequila-based cocktail. But use it sparingly, he cautions.

EIGHT: Match the weight of your food with the weight of your wine.

NINE: You can't go wrong going local. A Texas beer or wine with Texas barbecue. Go, Shiner Bock! A Shinn Estate Vineyard Cabernet Franc or Cabernet Sauvignon will marry beautifully with David Page's brisket (page 132). As it happens, Chef Page is married to Barbara Shinn and they are co-proprietors of this highly regarded, highly evolved Long Island biodynamic winery.

TEN: Some things are just meant to be. Bourbon and brisket. "Like peanut butter and jelly," says Sean McClure.

A LITTLE SCIENCE AND CHEMISTRY BEHIND SUCCESSFUL PAIRINGS

A. A fattier brisket goes with a wine higher in tannin. Tannins bind with proteins and fat and work together because—according to wine savant Scott Pactor, owner of Appellation Wine & Spirits in New York—tannin tends to dry your mouth out. (You know the feeling of biting into a grape seed?) This kind of dryness counteracts the rich fat of the brisket with pleasing results. An example of a wine high in tannin is a Cabernet Sauvignon or a Bordeaux.

B. A leaner brisket goes with a wine that's higher in acidity. Acidity, essentially, makes your mouth water. This acidity, says Scott, keeps your mouth nice and watery and keeps your palate feeling refreshed. Scott points out some terrific acidic wines like Barbera or Gamay in Cru Beaujolais.

C. From the Sword and Knife Chemistry Shorthand from the wine wordsmiths at thirtyfifty.co.uk: The proteins found in meat cut through tannins like a hot knife through butter. This results in softening the wine. As for acidic wine, the acidity cuts through dishes with lots of oil or fat, providing a refreshing sword.

D. A dark spirit that's high in acidity makes a great apéritif for the pre-brisket cocktail hour. Here, too, the acidity helps cut through the fat, gets the stomach juices flowing, and helps build an appetite. So a sidecar made with Cognac, Cointreau, and lemon juice, is a terrific choice.

Mile End. Tiny space, huge flavors, brilliantly reimagined Jewish comfort food.

> "Some American brown ales have notes of prune, apricot, and brown sugar —which just scream, 'Hey, brisket, with the tzimmes, marry me!'"

My own personal brisket liquidity started with me and award-winning Brooklyn Brewery brewmaster Garrett Oliver eating warm brisket sandwiches with deli mustard on rye at Mile End, the amazing Montreal-style deli that is making Boerum Hill, Brooklyn, feel like it's won the lottery. Why beer, I asked Garrett? Garrett loves—and is also an authority on—wine but says wine just can't echo all the flavors in a braised brisket that beer can. He tells me that the roasted and caramelized malt in beer grabs onto some of the same flavors in brisket. When it comes to taste harmony vs. contrast, Garrett is on the side of harmony. (I'm sure he's on the side of peace and love, too. He's a very gentle man.)

Garrett's specific suggestions: double bock–style beers, with their huge malty flavors. Double bocks are dark lagers, strong and full-bodied. They were originally brewed as liquid bread to sustain Bavarian monks while fasting. (A few thick slices of brisket in a South Carolina barbecue sauce would have done the same thing.) American brown ales are another of Garrett's recommendations. These are often described as "deeply flavored but not heavy," "intense," "potent." Some have notes of prune, apricot, and brown sugar—which just scream, "Hey, brisket, with the tzimmes (page 94), marry me!" Dark Belgian beers are a good choice with traditional braised briskets, since they, too, are complex and full of depth and character. A barbecue brisket with a spice rub works well with an India Pale Ale that balances an assertive bitterness with a burst of floral notes. Try a Belgian wheat beer with any braised brisket that has a fruit component—this beer has just the right sweetness to go with it. Coriander and orange peel add spicy, citrusy, nonsweet notes. Brian Van Flandern told me that a well-made stout or porter would work nicely with brisket. And he suggests cooking brisket in a hoppy IPA (India Pale Ale). Great flavor for the meat and a refreshing accompaniment. Chef Anita Lo, whose Brisket Noodle Soup is a kind of hybrid of unexpected and glorious flavors, recommends pairing her dish with a hoppy, fruity beer like a Green Flash's West Coast IPA. And Chef John Besh, true to his brisket and his community, suggests serving his dish with a cold Abita Beer from Abita Springs, Louisiana.

It was a different story when I discussed beer pairings with my friend Joe Clark, who studied in Munich and trained at the Kaltenberg Brewery with Prince Luitpold of Bavaria. Joe is the founder of The East Haddam Brewing Company in Connecticut. He is the smartest person I know and a stickler for doing it just so.

When I first asked Joe, he thought about beer/brisket pairings for a while and finally suggested that a really great Munich dark lager—like Koenig Ludwig Dunkel —which he helped make barrels of at Kaltenberg—would be the perfect match for barbecued brisket. Then a wonderful casual restaurant opened near where he lives, serving—among other things—slowly smoked, meltingly soft barbecue brisket with a sensational spicy rub and a lustrous sweet sauce, with a lightning bolt of chile to fire it up. After he ate there once, Joe came home and e-mailed me: "Oh, any good beer is going to be great with barbecue." So pick your favorite and go for it.

Same thing for wine. Pick what you like, which could be anything from Manischewitz to a $100 merlot. And if you don't have time to go to wine school (why don't you?) epicurious.com offers ideas for wine pairings with their brisket recipes. Any wine store will be happy to help. To make it even better, the totally wonderful, a brilliant, and meticulous Scott Pactor has taken most of the recipes in this book and given his suggestions for what goes with what. Thanks, Scott!

SCOTT'S TIPS: You can always use an inexpensive wine, but make it a good one. Find a small producer, off the beaten track. His suggestions are high/low or as he says, "luxurious/moderate."

MY TIP: Beer might be your first choice to go with the barbecue recipes, so most of those recipes are not included here.

1. A Seitan Brisket (page 11)

Scott says that with this fruit-forward (don't you love that term? I'm now using it all the time) brisket that's full of sweetness and spice, he's going for two lighter-bodied red wines. A juicy French with floral, fruity aromas. And an Italian lightly tannic Freisa.

High: Duboeuf Moulin-à-Vent
Low: La Casaccia Monferrato Freisa

2. Texas Oven-Roasted Beef Brisket (page 130)

This is barbecue flavor as big as the Texas ranch it came from. Scott suggests that a good match are two self-possessed wines with a peppery note, a dark fruit aroma, and good acidity.

High: a Côte-Rôtie, which has nice black pepper, dark fruit, and good acidity
Low: a Southern Rhone Syrah and Grenache blend

3. Temple Emanu-El Brisket (page 91)

There's so much dark fruit in this cranberry-caramelized brisket that Scott suggests a tannic wine that offers a stark contrast.

High: Domaine de Castel Jerusalem-Haute Judee (which is kosher)
Low: an '09 Ben Ami Merlot Galil (also kosher)

4. Grandma Ruby's Cholent (page 93)

A substantial, flavorful Jewish brisket dish deserves a wine that is rich, deep, and engaging.

High: Capcanes Peraj Petita Montsant (which is kosher)
Low: an '09 Ben Ami Merlot Galil (also kosher)

5. Nach Waxman's Brisket of Beef (page 110)

Scott recommends two Austrian wines that have black pepper and red fruit, which beautifully complement the tomato paste in the brisket.

High: '06 Beck Burg
Low: '08 Schreiner Blaufränkisch Burgenland

6. Classic Braised Beef Brisket (page 125)

Since the veal stock, mustard seeds, and peppers add some heft to this brisket, Scott suggests two bold, full-bodied American cabernets.

High: Heller Estate Carmel Valley Cabernet Sauvignon
Low: Old River Sierra Foothills Cabernet Sauvignon "Ponderosa Vineyard"

7. My Former Best Friend's Ex-Mother-in-Law's Brisket (page 90)

The acidity of the fresh white wines that Scott recommends cut through the onion soup. Both wines are biodynamically farmed. (As the contributor of this delicious but additive-packed recipe, I am so happy to compensate even the smallest bit with healthy eco-conscious wines.)

High: Colombia Toscano IGT Trebbiano/
      Malvasia blend
Low: Château Gaillard Touraine Sauvignon Blanc

8. Beef Brisket With Tangy Peaches (page 131)

Scott suggests two rich wines with a touch of sweetness to go with the tang (cinnamon, cloves, cider) of this special fruit brisket.

High: Maysara McMinnville Pinot Gris "Arsheen"
Low: Clément Klur Alsace "Gentil de Katz"
      Gerwurztraminer blend (it has the best
      label if you like cats)

9. My Favorite Brisket (page 105)

One nice rich brisket—two satisfying Chiantis. Scott remarks that each of these wines has both tannin and acidity and keeps the palate refreshed.

High: Riecine Chianti Classico
Low: Loacker Toscano Rosso IGT "Brillando"

10. Aunt Gladys's Brisket (page 92)

Here's a harmonious global pairing. The brisket, being very German in origin, mixes it up with two full-bodied wines—one from South Australia and one from Spain.

High: Walter Clappis Wine Co McLaren Vale
      Cabernet Sauvignon, "The Hedonist"
Low: Palin Colchagua Valley Carmenere

11. Cuban Creole Stew: Braised Beef Brisket with Fresh Chorizo and Squash (page 140)

Light wines with a good amount of acidity, says Scott, do better with spices than a more tannic wine would. And Chef Boulud's recipe already has acidity going, with the lime juice as an ingredient.

High: Montinore Willamette Valley Pinot Noir
Low: Hofer Niederosterreich Zweigelt

12. Braised Brisket with Tzimmes (page 94)

Cooking with cider? Why not drink some cider with your brisket? His other ingenious idea is the surprise and delight of matching this brisket with something sparkling. Brisket loves to be toasted.

High: Fleury Champagne Brut
Low: Bordelet Normany "Sidre Doux"
      Wild Card: Gruet Sparkling Wine from
      New Mexico

13. Braised Fresh Brisket in Stout with Onions (page 126)

Here, Scott says, maybe a beer would be in order, since this is a beer-braised brisket. If not, he picks two red wines that go well with stout, which is very like a dark chocolate beer. Both wines are deeply intense with a dark fruit aroma.

High: Trabucchi Amarone della Valpolicella "Cereolo"
Low: Schola Sarmenti Nardo "Roccamora"

14. Brisket in Sweet-and-Sour Sauce (page 127)

Scott likes a wine sweet enough to complement this yummy yin and yang dish —but with enough acidity not to be cloying. Let the Rieslings begin!

High: Hahnmuhle Nahe Riesling/Traminer blend
Low: Gysler Rheinhessen Riesling Kabinett "Weinheimer"

15. Aquavit Brisket (page 136)

There are so many outspoken spices in this bold, aromatic brisket that Scott suggests pairing it with wines that are much more subtle. In this case, Scott says, let the brisket shine. Takk, Scott!

High: Lemelson Willamette Valley Pinot Noir "Thea's Selection"
Low: Nittnaus Burgenland Blauer Zweigelt

16. Brisket in Tahina Sauce (page 135)

Tahina, while utterly delicious, is no delicate ingredient. So both the wines that Scott recommends have enough fruit and tannin to cut through the creaminess of the tahina. Why not lighten and brighten it up?

High: Paxton McLaren Vale Shiraz "Jones Block"
Low: Vinicola Real Rioja "Vina Los Valles"

17. Brisket Noodle Soup with Korean Chile (page 137)

There are so many wonderfully contrasting flavors and textures in this Asian-inspired brisket that Scott suggests two wines. Both have a lot of tannin and acid. Both contain the Nebbiolo grape.

High: Erbaluna Barolo "Vigna Rocche"

Sort-of-Low: Bianchi Gattinara "Vigneto Valferana"

18. My Mother's Brisket (page 96)

For this classic and simple brisket, straightforward wines are the way to go. Each has a fruit and tannic structure, says Scott. They pick up some of the pepper spice aroma of this brisket.

High: Frog's Leap Rutherford Merlot
Low: Aresti Chile Cabernet "Equilibrio"

19. Onion-Braised Beef Brisket (page 158)

This well-rounded brisket calls for a dry red. Scott found two beauties that fit the bill. The first is from Argentina (where they know a little something about beef) and the second is from Spain.

High: Santa Julia Mendoza Tempranillo
Low: La Rioja Alta Rioja Reserva "Ardanza"

20. Corned Beef with Parsley Sauce (page 141)

Corned beef is less fatty than a traditional braised brisket, so Scott suggests two pinot noirs. These wines have a good acid content and will keep the palate refreshed.

High: Kawarau Central Otago Pinot Noir
Low: Montinore Willamette Valley Pinot Noir

21. Sephardic Brisket (page 134)

Scott compares this brisket to a dark fruit compote. To pair with something this dominant, he suggests an easy-to-find chianti with some weight and acidity. And two Southern Italian wines that go wonderfully with the strong black tea in the sauce.

High: Chianti Classico
Low: Primitivo or Negroamaro

22. Slow Cooker Brisket (page 97)

This brisket gets slathered with barbecue sauce. Scott says that when it comes to finding a good wine pairing, a barbecue sauce is actually not so different from the big fruit components of other briskets. So both types profit from European red wines that boast some heft.

High: Ijalba Rioja "Graciano"
Low: Le Garrigon Côtes de Rhône

23. Brisket with Ginger, Orange Peel, and Tomato (page 128)

Scott notes that this brisket—with its sprightly orange peel, spring onions, and spices — suggests something Provençal. So his stylish wine selections add more fresh fruit pleasure.

High: Cantine del Notaio Aglianico del Vulture "Il Repertorio"
Low: Chateau de Roquefort Vin de France "Gueule de Loup"

24. Barbecued Brisket Sandwiches (with Firecracker Sauce) (page 132)

As noted in the introduction to this chapter, Chef Page recommends two of his favorite wines from his vineyard for these spicy sandwiches.

High: Shinn Estate Vineyard Cabernet Franc
Low: Shinn Estate Vineyard Cabernet Sauvignon

CLOVE'N HOOF COCKTAIL

Serves 1

This was created by the New York Times–praised Sean McClure, head mixologist at Tom Colicchio's Craft Restaurant in New York. Sean was formerly at the restaurant Daniel, so he has shaken and stirred it for the very best.

The Clove'N Hoof, says Sean, is the perfect drink for fall. Besides having the best name ever for the brisketphile, this is a drink that's nicely balanced, with rich deepness and a spicy aroma. The bourbon is infused with cloves and there are six spices (and counting!) that help compose the syrup that goes into it. So a Clove'N Hoof can both stand up to and complement a rich fatty meat like brisket that's always full of juicy flavor and usually enhanced by bold spices.

Why the name, I asked him? Sean told me it was inspired by the fact that Blanton's Bourbon, his bourbon of choice, has a horse logo on it. I think he means it was inspired by the fact that brisket deserves a very special drink.

1½ ounces **Clove-Infused Bourbon (recipe follows)**

½ ounce **Solerno Blood Orange Liqueur**

¼ ounce **Spiced Demerara Syrup (recipe follows)**

½ ounce **Carpano Punt e Mes**

½ ounce **freshly squeezed lemon juice**

For a chilled version, combine all the ingredients in a Boston shaker full of ice and shake vigorously. Serve over a 2-inch ice cube in an old fashioned glass.

For a warm cocktail: Combine all the ingredients except the lemon juice in a small metal pitcher, such as the kind used by baristas for steaming milk. Heat with a steam wand until hot to the touch.

Once heated, add the lemon juice, stir, pour into a snifter, and garnish with a flamed orange twist.

Clove-Infused Bourbon
Makes 1 liter

¼ cup whole cloves

1 liter bourbon (Blanton's Bourbon preferred)

In a quart-size container, combine the cloves and the bourbon. Reserve the bourbon bottle for later. Cover and shake well. Let sit for 20 to 30 minutes, tasting along the way. Once you have reached the desired intensity of the cloves, strain through a fine-mesh strainer and return to the original bottle.

Spiced Demerara Syrup
Makes 4 cups

2 tablespoons minced fresh orange zest

1 tablespoon whole cloves

5 cinnamon sticks

2 teaspoons freshly grated nutmeg

2 tablespoons diced fresh ginger

1 teaspoon whole peppercorns

8 whole allspice berries

8 cardamom pods

2 cups Demerara sugar

2 cups hot water

In a quart-size container, combine all of the ingredients. Stir until the sugar is completely dissolved. Let steep for 6 hours at room temperature, then cover and store in the refrigerator (leaving all the ingredients in the syrup).

Brisket: What a hunk.

11 The Amorous Brisket

"Nothing says 'I love you' like the breast of a cow
—or maybe that's diamonds…"

— *Jamie Geller, kosher.com founder*

There are times when the term brisket lover takes on new meaning. When "voluptuous," "juicy," "achingly tender," don't just describe the dish, but also the experience of sharing it with someone you love. And I'm not talking about watching the Super Bowl with your favorite cousin. The results of my personal experience and my copious research proves that I'm not the only romantic who's convinced that an excellent brisket can be far more seductive and swoonworthy than all the flowers and chocolates in the world. After all, you can't eat the freesia. Or braise the Godiva. One of the first things I found out was that while everyone is thrilled to talk about brisket, not everyone wants to talk about their sex lives. But even without contacting the Hilton or the Kardashian sisters, I managed to get some great stories and incontrovertible proof of brisket in the boudoir.

This guilty-pleasure confessional came to me from the funny and charming Jesse Kornbluth, a writer who lives in New York and edits the cultural concierge blog HeadButler.com:

JESSE KORNBLUTH: My Brisket Story

"It often happens—okay, it sometimes happens—that you and your new squeeze are having a fine dinner in a chic restaurant. The wine is velvet. A sense of well-being descends. So does lust. If only you could slip under the tablecloth and get to it. But you are not that kind of person. Dinner at her apartment? Different story.

"The brisket had cooked for so many hours that a knife was redundant. The wine was top-of-the-line California—it was the liquid equivalent of the brisket. The music was esoteric, soft but with a steady beat.

"One trick of great dining is small portions—and then seconds. We were on the second helping of brisket and the second bottle of wine when the conversation changed.

"The blouse and skirt came off. There was nothing underneath.
And that, kids, was just the preamble. Plates were pushed aside, glasses carefully moved. And up on the table she went, a treasure of a centerpiece.

"Ever since, at Katz's Deli, I order a brisket sandwich. I really like pastrami better, but with the brisket comes that memory. And it couldn't possibly be tastier."

"There are very few brisket recipes that do not have the word 'love' somewhere in their headnotes or descriptions."

Sigh. So that's the end of The Amorous Brisket chapter. Just kidding. If brisket didn't have the power to seduce, there wouldn't be what is called The Brisket Brigade in certain Jewish circles. (These circles, by the way, don't even admit there is such a thing.) Here's how The Brisket Brigade works. When a man is widowed, thoughtful neighbors and friends (read: unmarried women) console and comfort him the best way they know how: by dropping off a pot of still-warm, homemade brisket. With a heady cloud of steam drifting up into the air—all deep fragrance and heavenly flavor, well . . . it's enough to make a man think how nice it is to have a woman around the house. A loving, caring woman with a fine, deep pot and a brisket recipe. That approach is way too subtle for the likes of Laura Frankel, a cookbook writer and chef. In a you-go-girl JMag column, Ms. Frankel cautions singles: "Pay attention all you would-be brides . . . Brisket could make or break a marriage! . . . Show your brisket versatility and do both; you may just land prince charming." Do both what? Make and break your marriage? Oh, who cares? Ms. Frankel, who I assume is trying to add wit to her credentials, is on to something—acknowledging the power of brisket to help you find a Jewish Prince Charming.

Of course it would be a handsome French chef, the estimable Daniel Boulud, who really gets that a gently cooked brisket is both the quickest way and, paradoxically, the slowest way to someone's heart. "I always joke," he writes in *Braising*, "that braising is a good technique for newlyweds. It gives them plenty of time to pursue other things while their dinner cooks." It occurred to me that this side of brisket really is all about courtship and mating rituals. The Cultural Anthropology of Brisket. Brisket Gone Wild. It seems that mosquitoes, when they are courting, sing to each other in harmony. The male mosquito and the female mosquito keep modulating their musical frequencies as they get closer to consummating their relationship. Fruitflies (when they meet over the overripe bananas on your kitchen counter) attract each other with visual cues—the female flashes her little light to let the male know she's interested. And female bowerbirds who are looking to mate clearly signal their preference for male bowerbirds who have a large collection of blue objects.

Is that really so different from The Brisket Brigade signaling their intentions? Or one female blogger who has initiated certain successful rituals into her daily life—like smoking amazing barbecued ribs for her boyfriend. She says, "I had two ribs and my boyfriend ate the other 3½ pounds. He tells me that my ribs have deepened his love for me. Well, fine, but I know that just means he wants more ribs . . .)" I actually posted the question "Is brisket sexy?" (acknowledging that I was writing a book about it) on Serious Eats. One of the replies I got was "a fantastic brisket is dead sexy . . . any man who can make a good one could win my heart. More likely, my stomach." And I got this sweet reply: "Men are impressed by meat. More so by meat with gravy and mashed. Good luck to you."

" . . . braising is a good technique for newlyweds. It gives them plenty of time to pursue other things while their dinner cooks."

—*Chef Daniel Boulud*

Good luck to me, indeed. This book really took off when I acknowledged my passion for brisket at the same time I realized how passionate I was about passion. I wooed and won the love of my life (things had been moving a little slowly…) by making him my ethereal oh-so-sweet braised brisket with gravy-glazed carrots, along with a lusty, full-flavored Malbec the night he returned from a three-week business trip to Florida (think convention center, Applebee's, chain hotel, chain restaurants, rain, Olive Garden, room facing the interstate, Chuck E. Cheese's) . How could I fail? Gentle reader, I didn't. And for good measure, I upped the ante by serving tiny brioche rolls toasted to a golden crisp; the creamiest, dreamiest homemade macaroni and cheese ever; a warm molten dark chocolate cake with mint chocolate sauce, ringed by white chocolate–dipped strawberries. Afterward, a glass of well-aged Cognac. Welcome home, Eric!

For more scientific validation that, when it comes to brisket, all resistance is futile, I turned to a noted Berkeley psychotherapist whose practice includes couples counseling.

ME: "Is brisket the quickest way to a man's heart?"

DR. K: "Of course it is. It says you care. Brisket is a gift of love."

Brisket:
HOT!
HOT!
HOT!

1. Don't even think about serving the Weight Watchers brisket.

2. Ditto the Seitan Brisket unless you're both members of PETA.

3. Brisket + tasteful cleavage works every time.

4. Ask him if he likes mashed potatoes. With a lot of butter.

5. Tell her your idea of fun is watching someone break down beef.

6. Ixnay on serving the lean and possibly funky-tasting grass-fed brisket or any discussion about Michael Pollan or Temple Grandin.

7. Don't play any music that they play in the Apple Store. That means no Coldplay.

8. Tell him you make it all the time. And you'll always make it for him.

"You know what marriage is like at the start—all briskets and blow jobs...then it's downhill from there."

—adapted from the film Barney's Version

ME: (Happy sigh)

ME: "In your experience, is a brisket a bodice ripper kind of meat?" Can you use the words brisket and ecstasy in the same sentence?"

DR. K: "Brisket is a gentle passion. You just want to lie down afterward and cuddle. If you're that full and sated, you're lucky if you can make it to the bed."

I asked Nach Waxman, who is both a man of the world and a man of the brisket world.

ME: "Is brisket sexy?"

NACH: "It's hearty and comforting and served with love. It's slow speed sexy." But isn't every single thing that's good about brisket low and slow? And isn't it well worth waiting for?

Ask Eric.

12 Brisket Doesn't Stand Still

Going forward is good.
But with brisket, so is going backward.

Brisket, like any fine art form, is a work in progress. Sometimes the progress is good. Sometimes, not so good. Good would be the fact that so many chefs today are making transcendent hamburgers from brisket cuts. That would be everyone from Tyler Florence ("Have your butcher grind a piece of brisket. Mine has a 25- to 30-percent fat-to-meat ratio. It's gorgeous. It's my favorite.") to Chef/Owner Sam Howard in Portland, Maine to Chef Richard Blais in Atlanta (Flip Burger Boutique is one of *Bon Appétit's* 10 Best New Burger Spots, 2010). Brisket totally rocks the grill, thanks to a juicy jumbo brisket hot dog crafted by Michelin-starred Brooklyn chef Saul Bolton. Part of Bolton's new line of "Brooklyn Bangers," this pedigreed dog is two-thirds brisket, one-third pork fatback. Good would be Wagyu beef. Good would also be Certified Angus beef, heritage breeds like Piedmontese, the quality grass-fed beef that goes into a much loved burger at Spur Gastropub in Seattle, and anything from Niman Ranch.

For brisket today and in the future, Good would be a mission statement like that of Heritage Foods USA, who: "exist to promote genetic diversity, small family farms, and a fully traceable food supply. We are committed to making wholesome, delicious, and sustainably produced heritage foods available to

burgers in d if o a w ork so r

Who let the dogs out? Saul Bolton's Brooklyn Bangers, from left to right:
a brat, the famous brisket dog, a kielbasa, and a merguez.

all Americans. In doing so, we will foster the link between sustainable land use, small-scale food production, and preservation of the foods of past generations for future generations." Good would be a socially responsible butcher with a sense of humor. At the Chicago butcher shop Moo&Oink their funky meaty mission statement is: "Get your grill on!"

Good would be the news that brisket today is in the news—and making headlines! Not just in East Cupcake, but in the *New York Times*! Like this stop-the-presses lead: "This Little Brisket Went to Thailand." Okay, maybe it wasn't on the front page but it was the lead for a rave restaurant review of newly opened Kin Shop in Greenwich Village. The reviewer loved this soup: "The flavors are intense and specific, squid ink and the sesame oil, long beans and soft brisket, the squid itself and a chili fire . . ." The *Times* food critic Sam Sifton, who gets my vote for today's culinary Walt Whitman, characterizes Kin Shop as an American restaurant that uses Thai flavors: "a restaurant that nods at Thailand respectfully and uses its cuisine to fine effect." "Thai-ish."

Just a month later, here's another great *Times* review for the brisket at new French bistro Lyon: "Compliments should ring for the rich, heady steam and flavor of the restaurant's onion soup, thickened with brisket and made silky with a kind of marrow jam, flavored with fontina and a deep bass note of demi-glace."

Considering brisket respectfully and using its attributes to fine effect is leading to dazzling new global tastes and fusion triumphs at Kin Shop, at Lyon, at American Malaysian barbecue restaurants, at Dallas's Asador, which boasts "farm to fire" cooking, at Wexler's in San Francisco where diners enjoy barbecued Scotch eggs encrusted with fragrant smoked beef short rib ends that suggest deeply smoked brisket. Wexler's has also offered diners a Barbecued Brisket Bánh Mi with Pickled Cabbage, Fresno Chiles, Cilantro, Macaroni-Bacon Salad. And good is what *hasn't* changed. The brisket recipes that are made the same way year after year, for the same winter holiday, same summer picnic.

But what has changed? Here's a headline I never thought I'd see: "Where Cholent Is Chic." (Budapest, to be exact, where the young and the hip are riffing on cholent to great effect.) And in that same vein, good are older Jewish dishes in this country re-created with fresh artisanal fervor—and

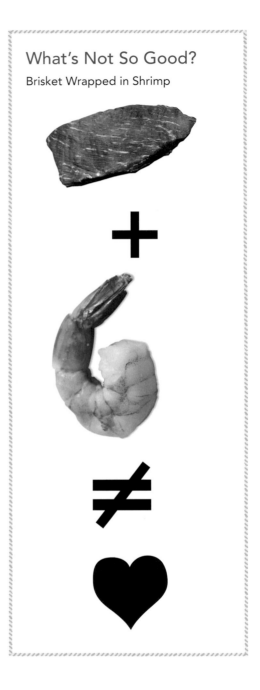

What's Not So Good?
Brisket Wrapped in Shrimp

flavor—by cooks like Noah Bernamoff at Brooklyn's Mile End delicatessen. Joan Nathan, noting this burgeoning movement, is impressed by Mr. Bernamoff's kasha varnishkes, a dish his mother made in his hometown of Montreal. Forget the perfectly adequate bow ties in the Wolff's box—Mr. Bernamoff "pinches dough into butterfly shapes by hand." Doing nothing less, Ms. Nathan notes, than "reinventing this Eastern European comfort dish in what he thinks might be the tradition of his ancestors." On the barbecue side, brisket gets treated with respect today in competitions, cook-offs, cookbooks. Its proper preparation is taught at barbecue schools, culinary institutes, universities. One of the best is Paul (aka Kansas City Baron of Barbecue) Kirk's school for aspiring pit masters.

So what's not so good? Well, I'd say some well-intentioned brisket misses/messes, such as "Brisket Wrapped in Shrimp," a surf and turf appetizer conjured up by an intrepid food blogger. Would it surprise you if I told you the name of this blog is *Cooking by the Seat of My Pants*? "Oh, my goodness," says my friend Marsha Dick, when I tell her about this neo-beef/shellfish combination. Marsha grew up kosher and was tactful enough to simply comment, "It doesn't appeal to me." I don't think you have to grow up kosher to have your doubts. What's next? Brisket scampi? Not so good would also be a beef brisket Christmas appetizer I found online (somehow nothing in that phrase sounds appetizing), layered brisket breakfast casseroles, the worthy Jews for Jesus brisket recipe, synthetic Liquid Smoke, a festering special interest group on Facebook called PARM (People Against Red Meat).

What else is new? More attempts at humor. Some LOL, some not so great. Brisket humor—like mother-in-law jokes—can be tricky. I did laugh when I saw there's a barbecue competition team called You've Been Served. But I'm not amused by a Food Network show titled *Two Goys, a Girl, and a Brisket*. Then there's newly aggressive brisket marketing, like the relentlessly advertised and super annoying Bubbie Jeanne's All-Purpose Brisket Magic Cooking Sauce, which is, according to seemingly fictitious Bubbie Jeanne, "The world's best brisket sauce." Says who? An unintentionally funny rave for Bubbie Jeanne on her homepage: "When my family tasted the meat, they looked around to see if Grandma had returned to make just one more brisket! Ann G."

Oh, Ann, she's dead. Get over it. Maybe it's me and bubbes. My other strong dislike on the contemporary brisket front is likeable octogenarian home cook Bayla "Bubbe" Scher. Thanks to her techno-savvy brand-building media-hungry grandson (and I say that with all due respect) Avrom Honig, this real-life bubbe, hosts a Jewish cooking podcast with the creepy title of "Feed Me Bubbe" from her kitchen in Worcester, Massachusetts. Maybe I should just be content that people want to broadcast their briskets, serve them with eggnog, send Bubbie Jeanne's kids to college.

So while it's new and improved, brisket is also old and improved. That's the beautifully complex nature of this very simple cut. When you get right down to it, brisket has to do with life: remembering it, sharing it, celebrating it.

"Oh juicy, tender, savory perfection, where have you been all my life?"

—*Anonymous brisket eater*

Acknowledgments

To Andrews McMeel, LLC, the publisher that restores this author's faith in publishing. What a team—smart, savvy, pragmatic, professional, dedicated, enthusiastic, and brisket lovers all. Thanks especially to Kirsty Melville, Lane Butler, and Tammie Barker.

To Kathy Brennan, who worked with me from day one, recipe one. Kathy's incredibly high standards and determination to make the best waaaay better raised the bar. Somehow a brisket just knew that Kathy expected a lot from it.

To Happy Menocal, whose design skills are extraordinary and who is as artful as a girl can be. Only Happy could go from Ellis Island to Julia Child to a chef in the buff to a dab of miso with such brio and style.

To Amy Lundeen, without whom we would not have great shots, Le Creuset pots, archival treasures, Big Green Eggs, and exactly the right bottle of red wine at exactly the right angle.

To Ardie Davis, who introduced me to Kansas City brisket, who shared his phenomenal barbecue photos, and who answered every question I asked him with grace and good humor. Two thousand e-mails and counting . . .

To Steve Sheppard and Lisa Digernes for their always wise legal guidance. And for lending me Andreas Viestad and Brian Perrone.

To the brilliant community of masters and makers who make the best of brisket:

Michael Pollan, Joan Nathan, Anita Lo, Nach Waxman, Robb Walsh, Richard Blais, John Besh, John T. Edge, J. Kenzi Lopez-Alt, Guy Crosby, Paul Kirk, Colman Andrews, Ari Weinzweig, Alex Young, Seamus Mullen, Daniel Boulud, David Tanis, Erin McMurrer, Chris Kimball, Christine Smith, Noah Bernamoff, Rae Cohen,

Josh Baum, Sam Hayward, David Page, Barbara Shinn, Andreas Viestad, Maura McEvoy, Tammie Barker, Daniel Rose, Lisa Rose, Matt Sartwell, Kryspin Moleda, Tom Perini, Lisa Perini, Susan Cannan, Tom Mylan, T. J. Burnham, Patrick Martin, Erica Helms, Brian Perrone, Tommy York, Matthew Morgan, Colin Clark, "Meathead"(aka Barbecue God), Gil Marks, Richard Westhaver, Robbie Richter, Zak Pelaccio, John Shields, Sara Moulton, Frances Lam, Anatoly Liberman, Tony Schatzie, Dalia Carmel, Nicolette Hahn Niman, Adam Schuman, Saul Bolton, Garrett Oliver, Sean McClure, Brian Van Flandern, Scott Pactor, Joe Clark, Corby Kummer, Todd Gray, Ellen Kassoff Gray, Levana Kirschenbaum, Simon Hopkinson, Niman Ranch, Jim Cohen, Jean Anderson, Jane Ziegelman, Fergus Henderson, Hugh Fearnley-Whittingstal, Chuck Madonna, Holland Court Market, Marlow & Daughters.

And to all the brisket cheerleaders and brisketwise:

Jesse Kornbluth, Abby Shulman Palmer, Daniel S. Palmer, Dan Fromson, Razonia McClellan, Sol Slotnik, Diane Reverand, Meira Goldberg, Ellen Silver, Thelma Silver, Minna and Frank Ramson, Jodi Badagliacca, Daphne Hurford, Sandy Padwe, Cindy Suozzi, Ray Basso, Annette Mark, Michael Mark, Wendy Mark, Ruth Friendly, Katharine Barnwell, Rabbi David Posner, Kelly Alexander, Eddie Gehman Kohan, Semonti M. Stephens, Martin Eidelburg, James Yeh, Kate Telfeyan, Rosalie McCabe, Ivo Jamrosz, Jo Ann Volk Lederman, Patty Volk, Mandy Moore, Liz Errico, Regina Matthews, Colleen Jezersek, Mary Gwynn, Melissa Bachrach, Phyllis Cohen, Jeri Kronen, Mike Steinberger, John Swansburg, Barbara Kafka, Roberta Greenberg, Jennifer McGruther, Esther Bushell, Liz Errico, Abigail Connell, Michael Osler, the Cosmopolitan Club Bulletinettes, the Thursday 9:15 Pilates class.

Special literary thanks to James Yeh for sharing an excerpt from "On Meat over Meat: Dinner with Gary Shteyngart," originally published in *Gigantic* #1, 2009.

A musical note to thank Rhett & Link & The Homestead Pickers for "The BBQ Song" http://www.youtube.com/watch?v=6ubTQfr_tyY

For "The Last Brisket" joke, thanks to David Minkoff.

Image Credits

Roger Sherman, pp. vi, x, xv, 3, 20, 25, 26, 31, 45, 48, 51, 68, 75, 104, 106 (top), 108, 109, 111, 133, 137, 139, 148–149, 150, 152–153, 155, 156, 160, 169, 170, 173, 174, 175

Paul Haight, p. ix

Le Creuset, p. xii

James Stevenson, © The Cartoon Bank, CondeNast.com, p. xvi

Matt Stoller, p. 5

Steven Weinberger, p. 6

Robert Landau/Alamy, p. 7

Sara Proietti, p. 8

Meathead, AmazingRibs.com, pp. 12, 67

Franceeco Tonelli, p. 14

John Farnan, p. 19

Jack Daniel's, p. 29

John Anderson, p. 32

Colin Clark, p. 54

Fatty Crew, p. 58

Rebs Demling, p. 64, 78

Robert Weber, © The Cartoon Bank, CondeNast.com, p. 81

Maura McEvoy, p. 82, 121,

Joan Nathan, pp. 102–103

Matt Sartwell, 106 (bottom)

The Waxman Family, p. 107

Ardie Davis, p. 116, 119, 164, 167

F. Mako Koiwai, p. 122

Equinox Restaurant, p. 127

Owen Franken, p. 130

Our Labor of Love, p. 142, 143

Russell French, 145

Rae Cohen, p. 181

Solomon Krueger, p. 193

Adam Schneider, p. 196

****NO CREDITS, pp. 34, 52, 63, 73, 84, 87, 88, 90, 92, 95, 125, 129, 134, 135, 136, 141, 162-163, 177, 188****

Metric Conversions and Equivalents

Metric Conversion Formulas

To Convert	Multiply
Ounces to grams	Ounces by 28.35
Pounds to kilograms	Pounds by .454
Teaspoons to milliliters	Teaspoons by 4.93
Tablespoons to milliliters	Tablespoons by 14.79
Fluid ounces to milliliters	Fluid ounces by 29.57
Cups to milliliters	Cups by 236.59
Cups to liters	Cups by .236
Pints to liters	Pints by .473
Quarts to liters	Quarts by .946
Gallons to liters	Gallons by 3.785
Inches to centimeters	Inches by 2.54

Approximate Metric Equivalents

Weight

¼ ounce	7 grams
½ ounce	14 grams
¾ ounce	21 grams
1 ounce	28 grams
1¼ ounces	35 grams
1½ ounces	42.5 grams
1⅔ ounces	45 grams
2 ounces	57 grams
3 ounces	85 grams
4 ounces (¼ pound)	113 grams
5 ounces	142 grams
6 ounces	170 grams
7 ounces	198 grams
8 ounces (½ pound)	227 grams
16 ounces (1 pound)	454 grams
35.25 ounces (2.2 pounds)	1 kilogram

Volume

¼ teaspoon	1 milliliter
½ teaspoon	2.5 milliliters
¾ teaspoon	4 milliliters
1 teaspoon	5 milliliters
1¼ teaspoons	6 milliliters
1½ teaspoons	7.5 milliliters
1¾ teaspoons	8.5 milliliters
2 teaspoons	10 milliliters
1 tablespoon (½ fluid ounce)	15 milliliters
2 tablespoons (1 fluid ounce)	30 milliliters
¼ cup	60 milliliters
⅓ cup	80 milliliters
½ cup (4 fluid ounces)	120 milliliters
⅔ cup	160 milliliters
¾ cup	180 milliliters
1 cup (8 fluid ounces)	240 milliliters
1¼ cups	300 milliliters
1½ cups (12 fluid ounces)	360 milliliters
1⅔ cups	400 milliliters
2 cups (1 pint)	460 milliliters
3 cups	700 milliliters
4 cups (1 quart)	.95 liter
1 quart plus ¼ cup	1 liter
4 quarts (1 gallon)	3.8 liters

Length

⅛ inch	3 millimeters
¼ inch	6 millimeters
½ inch	1¼ centimeters
1 inch	2½ centimeters
2 inches	5 centimeters
2½ inches	6 centimeters
4 inches	10 centimeters
5 inches	13 centimeters
6 inches	15¼ centimeters
12 inches (1 foot)	30 centimeters

Oven Temperatures

To convert Fahrenheit to Celsius, subtract 32 from Fahrenheit, multiply the result by 5, then divide by 9.

Description	Fahrenheit	Celsius	British Gas Mark
Very cool	200°	95°	0
Very cool	225°	110°	¼
Very cool	250°	120°	½
Cool	275°	135°	1
Cool	300°	150°	2
Warm	325°	165°	3
Moderate	350°	175°	4
Moderately hot	375°	190°	5
Fairly hot	400°	200°	6
Hot	425°	220°	7
Very hot	450°	230°	8
Very hot	475°	245°	9

Common Ingredients and Their Approximate Equivalents

1 cup uncooked rice = 225 grams

1 cup all-purpose flour = 140 grams

1 stick butter (4 ounces • ½ cup • 8 tablespoons) = 110 grams

1 cup butter (8 ounces • 2 sticks • 16 tablespoons) = 220 grams

1 cup brown sugar, firmly packed = 225 grams

1 cup granulated sugar = 200 grams

Information compiled from a variety of sources, including Recipes into Type *by Joan Whitman and Dolores Simon (Newton, MA: Biscuit Books, 2000);* The New Food Lover's Companion *by Sharon Tyler Herbst (Hauppauge, NY: Barron's, 1995); and* Rosemary Brown's Big Kitchen Instruction Book *(Kansas City, MO: Andrews McMeel, 1998).*

Index